THE

POEMS

OF

ALFRED B. STREET.

IN TWO VOLUMES.

VOL. I.

NEW YORK:
PUBLISHED BY HURD AND HOUGHTON,
459 BROOME STREET.
1867.

RIVERSIDE, CAMBRIDGE:
STEREOTYPED AND PRINTED BY
H. O. HOUGHTON AND COMPANY.

CONTENTS OF VOLUME I.

POEMS.

THE GRAY FOREST EAGLE.

WITH storm-daring pinion, and sun-gazing eye,
The Gray Forest Eagle is king of the sky!
Oh, little he loves the green valley of flowers,
Where sunshine and song cheer the bright summer hours,
He hears in those haunts only music, and sees
But rippling of waters and waving of trees;
There the red robin warbles, the oriole swings,
And the thrasher thrills deep the whole wood as it sings;
And if those proud pinions, perchance, sweep along,
There is shrouding of plumage, a hushing of song;
The sunlight falls stilly on leaf and on moss,
With only his shadow black gliding across;
But the dark, gloomy gorge, where down plunges the foam
Of the fierce, rocky torrent, he claims as his home.

There he blends his keen shriek with the roar of the flood,
And the many-voiced sounds of the blast-smitten wood;
From the fir's lofty summit, where morn hangs its wreath,
He views the mad waters white writhing beneath.
On a limb of that moss-bearded hemlock far down,
With bright azure mantle, and gay mottled crown,
The kingfisher watches, while o'er him his foe,
The fierce hawk, sails circling, each moment more low.
Now poised are those pinions and pointed that beak,
His dread swoop is ready, when hark! with a shriek,
His eyeballs red-blazing, high bristling his crest,
His snaky neck arched, talons drawn to his breast,
With the rush of the wind-gust, the glancing of light,
The Gray Forest Eagle shoots down in his flight.
One blow of those talons, one plunge of that neck,
The strong hawk hangs lifeless, a blood-dripping wreck;
And as dives the free kingfisher, dart-like on high
With his prey soars the Eagle, and melts in the sky.

A fitful red glaring, a low rumbling jar,
Proclaim the Storm-Demon, yet raging afar;
The black cloud strides upward, the lightning more red,
And the roll of the thunder, more deep and more dread;
A thick pall of darkness is cast o'er the air,
And on bounds the blast with a howl from its lair.
The lightning darts zigzag and forked through the gloom,
And the bolt launches o'er with crash, rattle, and boom;

The Gray Forest Eagle, where, where has he sped?
Does he shrink to his eyrie, and shiver with dread?
Does the glare blind his eye? Has the terrible blast
On the wing of the Sky-King a fear-fetter cast?
No no, the brave Eagle! he thinks not of fright;
The wrath of the tempest but rouses delight.
To the flash of the lightning his eye casts a gleam;
To the shriek of the wild blast he echoes his scream;
And with front like a warrior that speeds to the fray,
And a clapping of pinions, he 's up and away!
Away, oh, away, soars the fearless and free!
What recks he the sky's strife? — its monarch is he!
The lightning darts round him, undaunted his sight;
The blast sweeps against him, unwavered his flight;
High upward, still upward he wheels, till his form
Is lost in the black scowling gloom of the storm.

The tempest glides o'er with its terrible train,
And the splendor of sunshine is glowing again;
Again smiles the soft, tender blue of the sky,
Waked bird-voices warble, fanned leaf-voices sigh;
On the green grass dance shadows, streams sparkle
and run,
The breeze bears the odor its blossom-kiss won,
And full on the form of the Demon in flight
The rainbow's magnificence gladdens the sight!
The Gray Forest Eagle! oh, where is he now,
While the sky wears the smile of its God on its brow?
There 's a dark, floating spot by yon cloud's pearly
wreath,

With the speed of the arrow 'tis shooting beneath;
Down, nearer and nearer it draws to the gaze,
Now over the rainbow, now blent with its blaze,
To a shape it expands, still it plunges through air,
A proud crest, a fierce eye, a broad wing are there;
The Eagle — the Gray Forest Eagle — once more
He sweeps to his eyrie: his journey is o'er!

Time whirls round his circle, his years roll away,
But the Gray Forest Eagle minds little his sway;
The child spurns its buds for Youth's thorn-hidden bloom,
Seeks Manhood's bright phantoms, finds Age and a tomb;
But the Eagle's eye dims not, his wing is unbowed,
Still drinks he the sunshine, still scales he the cloud!

The green tiny pine-shrub points up from the moss,
The wren's foot would cover it, tripping across;
The beech-nut, down dropping, would crush it beneath,
But 'tis warmed with heaven's sunshine, and fanned by its breath;
The seasons fly past it, its head is on high,
Its thick branches challenge each mood of the sky;
On its rough bark the moss a green mantle creates,
And the deer from his antlers the velvet-down grates;
Time withers its roots, it lifts sadly in air
A trunk dry and wasted, a top jagged and bare,
Till it rocks in the soft breeze, and crashes to earth,
Its brown fragments strewing the place of its birth.

The Eagle has seen it up-struggling to sight,
He has seen it defying the storm in its might,
Then prostrate, soil-blended, with plants sprouting o'er,
But the Gray Forest Eagle is still as of yore.
His flaming eye dims not, his wing is unbowed,
Still drinks he the sunshine, still scales he the cloud!

He has seen from his eyrie the forest below
In bud and in leaf, robed with crimson and snow;
The thickets, deep wolf-lairs, the high crag his throne,
And the shriek of the panther has answer'd his own.
He has seen the wild red man the lord of the shades,
And the smoke of his wigwams curled thick in the glades;
He has seen the proud forest melt, breath-like, away,
And the breast of the earth lying bare to the day;
He sees the green meadow-grass hiding the lair,
And his crag throne spread naked to sun and to air;
And his shriek is now answer'd, while sweeping along,
By the low of the herd and the husbandman's song;
He has seen the wild red man swept off by his foes,
And he sees dome and roof where those smokes once arose;
But his flaming eye dims not, his wing is unbowed,
Still drinks he the sunshine, still scales he the cloud!

An emblem of Freedom, — stern, haughty, and high, —
Is the Gray Forest Eagle, that king of the sky!
It scorns the bright scenes, the gay places of earth;
By the mountain and torrent it springs into birth;

There rocked by the wild wind, baptized in the foam,
It is guarded and cherished, and there is its home!
When its shadow steals black o'er the empires of kings,
Deep terror, deep heart-shaking terror, it brings;
Where wicked oppression is armed for the weak,
There rustles its pinion, there echoes its shriek;
Its eye flames with vengeance, it sweeps on its way,
And its talons are bathed in the blood of its prey.

Oh, that Eagle of Freedom! when cloud upon cloud
Swathed the sky of my own native land with a shroud, —
When lightnings gleamed fiercely, and thunderbolts rung, —
How proud to the tempest those pinions were flung!
Though the wild blast of battle rushed fierce through the air
With darkness and dread, still the Eagle was there;
Unquailing, still speeding, his swift flight was on,
Till the rainbow of Peace crowned the victory won.

Oh, that Eagle of Freedom! age dims not his eye,
He has seen Earth's mortality spring, bloom, and die!
He has seen the strong nations rise, flourish, and fall,
He mocks at time's changes, he triumphs o'er all;
He has seen our own land with wild forests o'er-spread,
He sees it with sunshine and joy on its head;
And his presence will bless this, his own chosen clime,
Till the Archangel's mandate is set upon Time.

NATURE.

NATURE, faint emblem of Omnipotence,
Shaped by His hand, the shadow of His light,
The veil in which He wraps His majesty,
And through whose mantling folds He deigns to
 show,
Of His mysterious, awful attributes
And dazzling splendors, all man's feeble thought
Can grasp uncrushed, or vision bear unquenched,—
She is the shrine of this, my offering-song.

God glanced on chaos, into form it sprang;
Worlds clustered round Him; instant at His will,
Blazing, they darted to their destined spheres,
Spangling the void, and in their orbits wheeled,
Each with a different glory. Kindled suns
Shot their fierce beams, and gentle moons were robed
In soft, pure, silvery lustre. Chaos lived.

As the bright shapes were speeding to their goals
The Angels gazed with wonder. Orb on orb
Swept past their vision, shedding fitful gleams
Upon their jewelled brows and rainbow wings,

And trailing, as they whirled along their flight,
Pathways of splendor, till the boundless space
Flashed in a web of gorgeous brilliancy.
But when Omnipotence had formed His robe,
And cast its spangled blazonry round Heaven,
The countless myriads of those shining ones,
Their wonder changed to awe, bowed crown and harp
Before the dazzling brightness. Then, as stole
The first low music of the singing-stars
Swelling and spreading through the gleaming space,
The glittering ranks, their awe to gladness turned,
Leaping erect, poured from the quivering string
Their anthem to the Holiest, till Heaven's air,
Stirred by the diapason of the hymn,
Rolled on, an ocean of deep billowy sounds.

At the creative summons, Earth had wheeled
In her eternal course ; — oh ! not as now,
Marred by the bitter curse that flowed from sin,
Scathed by God's justice, darkened with His wrath,
And made more black by man, — but pure and sweet
In all the beauty of her blossoming youth,
In all the fragrance of her new-born spring.
Paradise, rising at its Maker's touch,
Bloomed in its loveliness ; the glossy leaves
Roofed the rich grass with emerald ; gorgeous flowers
Swung incense to the air, and warbling birds
And rippling waters made each wind that breathed
A wandering tongue of softest melody.

Alas! that sin should blight that Paradise!
Woe for the brightness vanished from the earth!
Woe for lost Eden! As the fiery sword
Gleamed before eyes that never more might view
The glories passed away with innocence,
Heaven's radiant brows grew pale at all the grief
The first transgression then entailed on man.

Steeped in her wickedness, Earth revelled on.
At length God's anger burst. The mighty rains
Dashed, torrent-like, from black and scowling skies
That veiled the world with darkness: valleys swelled
To leaping rivers, plains to dashing lakes,
And gorges to mad plunging cataracts;
The peopled city and the lonely cot
Sank in the rising waters; mountain peaks,
Dotting the billowy desert, were o'erwhelmed,
Until a boundless ocean wildly tossed
Its giant surges, and with ceaseless roar
Thundered its requiem o'er a world destroyed.

Borne by the dove o'er this mysterious sea,
To anxious eyes within the floating Ark,
The gladdening olive-branch gave pledge of hope
And sure deliverance.

And when that bright bird,
Darting through breaking gloom, o'er lessening flood,
Vanished forever, fainter fell the roar,
Till the dread requiem ceased; the watery veil

Shrank from Earth's features, and, her baptism o'er,
In the pure sunshine she looked up and smiled;
While o'er her freshened beauty, delicate hues
Glowed in arched brightness on the fleeting clouds, —
God's type of mercy and averted wrath.
Time has rolled on his rapid flood since then —
Each wave a century — towards that barrier
O'er which it leaps, a mighty cataract,
Into the ocean of Eternity.
Myriads of human motes have sported o'er
Its boiling surges, and been swept away;
Formed of its mists, upon its slippery banks
Empires have risen and vanished; battle-fields
Have mingled with its flow their crimson stains,
And epochs ruffled it in spots to foam.
Nature has kept her order, high above
The wild mutations of this rolling tide.
Twin-born with Time, and twin-existent, naught
Shall swerve her from her proud, sublime career,
Until the day of the dread holocaust,
When the red sky shall shrivel like a scroll
Before the splendors of that "great white throne"
Blazing mid crashing spheres and shuddering worlds.

How countless and how multiform the scenes
Nature presents, expanding as we tread
Her sacred precincts! With what various tongues
She teaches, and how vast the wisdom gained!

Show we her scenes, in Europe's differing climes,

Asia the gorgeous, stricken Africa,
And God's most glorious gift, — our own wild land.

An English landscape: a green winding lane,
Skirted with fragrant hawthorns, casting down
Broad stripes of shadow on the pleasant grass,
Streaked by the slant rays of the sinking sun;
The mown hay's odor fills the balmy air,
And the light clanging of the whetted scythe
Rings from the meadow; o'er yon grove of oaks,
Tufting the sky with dome-like foliage,
Points the mossed steeple of the village church;
And through the parted edges of the leaves
Gleam the white gravestones: by this cottage-porch
Stoops the rough cart, its long tongue thrust to earth,
And near it crouches the tired, panting ox,
With the grim mastiff, growling in his sleep.
Beneath the woodbined lattice, flashing back
In dazzling sparks the sunshine, the faint hum
Of the whirled spinning-wheel is blending sweet
With the deep low of the approaching kine,
And the shrill creaking of the harvest-wain;
O'er the green wave of meadow, melting dim
In the far distance, sweeps the lordly park,
With its gray ivied castle, haughtily
Frowning with tower and wall and battlement.

A scene of glorious Italy! the sky —
A delicate sapphire — smiles o'er silvered slopes
Bright with the olive; purpled terraces

Rich with the grape. Isle-dotted Como winds
To the dim shroud of its horizon-mist.
The glossy myrtles in the fanning air
Cast rapid glitterings. In the sunlight, gleam
A prostrate column and a broken arch,
Their marble bathed in gold: while far, the Alps
Lift their proud monarch-forms, with regal robes
Of forest purple, — dazzling diamond crowns,
And craggy sceptres, — guarding, with stern looks,
The radiant climes that brighten at their feet.

Romantic Switzerland! wild mountain peaks
Casting gigantic shadows, their grim shapes
Streaked with bright silver, the high, headlong plunge
Of foaming torrents; from its crag, the fir
Leans o'er the cloven gorge with gloomy frown,
While the slight poplar and the graceful larch
Cluster round chalets set, like spotted pearls,
Upon the bosoms of the billowy hills.
The glacier flings its darts of dazzling light
In the broad sun; and towering up, Mont Blanc
Throws down the mighty mantle of his shade
Upon the vassal-mountains crouching round.

The scorching noontide sun of India fires
The sandal-scented air. The tall bamboo
Walls the bright Ganges with its jointed stems;
Motionless droops the tamarind in the heat,
While looming far, the trunk-linked banyan spreads
Its branching columns and its leafy aisles, —

A templed forest. On his crashing path
Through the down-trampled canes, the elephant
Treads to the dark, cool portal, and is lost
In the wide-spreading shadow. To the clear,
Lily-wreathed mirror of the sacred flood,
Bends the striped tiger, and then crouching, hides
Within the matted jungle; while around
The tall pagoda and the sculptured mosque
The fig is bursting, and the cocoa hangs
High in the glowing air its ripening globes.

Africa shows her picture. Limitless
Spread the gray sands, which in their mighty march,
Grain upon grain, — each toilsome stride an age, —
Have whelmed magnificent temple, palace proud,
And gorgeous city, and still onward move, —
Their only witnesses, the myriad years
That o'er have flown, since, slow and deep and still,
But awful in their stillness, they have passed.
Afar upon the blue, the pyramid
Towering cuts sharply; near it frowns the Sphynx
Wrapped in its sandy mantle, while beneath
The grateful shadow of its guardian-palm,
The tremulous silver of the fountain glows;
Caravan-camels are reclining round
Mid turbaned groups. Quick, skimming like a dart,
Speeds the light antelope. But what wild shapes
Are bursting from the far horizon's rim?
High towering as they come, the pillared sands,
With fearful roaring and with furnace-breath,

Shrivelling and scorching, whirl along their course :
Brass glares above ; red surges toss below ;
And where they pass, the fierce hyena delves
And howls in triumph as he rends his prey.

America, with her rich, green forest-robe !
Yon eagle sweeping from his sunward path,
Stoops his broad pinion to a towering peak ;
Far as on every side his keen eye darts,
An emerald ocean stretches, and its depths,
Formed by the leaves, as ocean by its drops,
Are lying motionless in breathless sleep ;
But the free, viewless wind sweeps over them ;
They toss in flashing billows, while a sound
Arises, swelling in full, deep-toned strength,
The playful gambols of this boundless sea,
The murmurs of its gladness. Now a cloud,
Massive and black, strides up ; the angry gleam
Of the red lightning cleaves the frowning folds,
And the far thunder mutters ; then, as glare
Opens on glare and crash succeeds to crash,
An awful roar comes deepening ; 't is the wrath
Of the fierce whirlwind darting on its way,
Crushing beneath its tread gigantic trees,
Leaving its broad strewed path — a yawning chasm —
Through the deep forest-heart : then, as uplifts
The scowling curtain of the storm, and leaps
The sunshine in the coverts, from his lair
Bounds the scared panther with his ringing shriek,
And from his swampy den the startled wolf

Springs with his clicking teeth and savage snarl;
The forest glitters and sends forth a burst
Of music, and upon the mossy glade
Light treads the graceful deer: the landscape smiles.

What splendid beauty, and what grandeur wild
Nature displays in this, her loveliest clime, —
This diamond of her casket! With one hand
She grasps the pine among its mantled snow,
Rocking in Winter's blasts; the other holds
The orange blossoming mid its golden fruit,
And trembling in the odor-bearing wind
Of changeless Summer. Here, her sloping brows
Smile in the bathing sunshine; towering, there,
They wear the stern black clouds like diadems;
Her veins — the glorious rivers rolling on,
Now dashing wild o'er barrier-ice, and now
Rippling beneath magnolian chalices;
Her eyes — the sea-like lakes, whose angry tones
Vie with the ocean-thunder; and her robe —
The gorgeous foliage of the mighty woods.

Not only is she grand and beautiful
In her majestic outlines, but she paints
With every passing season's varying brush
Fairy-like pictures of bright loveliness.

Joy throughout Nature. April's fitful smiles
Have yielded to the warm, soft looks of May.
The hopple and the cherry smile no more

In white bouquets. The glossy down has left
The beech-sprays, and the perfumed birch has dropped
Its delicate tassels on the brightened moss.
Alone the dogwood shows its blossoms now,
Stars of white gauze outspread o'er every leaf,
Breaking upon the eye amid the young
Transparent verdure spotted on the boughs,
Spreading as each day brings a kindlier sun.
In the moist hollows and by streamlet-sides
The grass stands thickly. Sunny banks have burst
Into blue sheets of scented violets.
The woodland warbles, and the noisy swamp
Has deepened in its tones. All speak of hope,
Of renovated youth, and coming joy.

A day in June: the full-grown canopy-leaves
Sketch, in the gentle breathings of the air,
Black quivering forms upon the flower-gemmed earth.
O'er the branch-sheltered stream the laurel hangs
Its gorgeous clusters, and the basswood breathes
From its pearl-blossoms, fragrance. Swinging light
Upon the hemlock-top, the thrasher sounds
His three-toned flute. From her cool shadowy nook
The doe has led her dappled fawn, to taste
The low, sweet glade-grass with its clover-spots.
Bees waft their lyres; clouds wreathe and melt above,
And sunshine smiles in golden gloss below.
But now the wind stirs freshlier; darting round,
The spider tightens his frail web; dead leaves

Whirl in quick eddies from the mounds; the snail
Creeps to its twisted fortress, and the bird
Crouches amid its feathers. Wafted up,
The stealing cloud with soft gray blinds the sky,
And in its vapory mantle, onward steps
The summer shower; over the shivering grass
It merrily dances, rings its tinkling bells
Upon the dimpling stream, and moving on,
It treads upon the leaves with pattering feet
And softly murmured music. Off it glides;
And as its misty robe lifts up, and melts,
The sunshine darting with a sudden burst,
Strikes o'er the scene a magic brilliancy.
A damp, fresh fragrance from bathed leaves and flowers
Steeps the cool, pleasant air. Tree speaks to tree
In mirthful warbles; the wet bushes chirp,
And the grass answers with its insect-tones.

Gorgeous October! at the reddening morn
Breathes a slight chillness through the bracing air.
The white-frost sparkles, showing myriad prints
Of the wood-wanderers, and the beaded drops
Glitter upon the gossamer. As the skirt
Of rivulet-mist fades gently in the sky,
Rich scenes of varied splendor beam around.
A forest carnival! as though the threads
Of the sun's light had melted on the leaves
Each with its different hue; as though all tints
Of gem, of bird, of flower, of cloud, of sky,
Had met and blended in a general glow.

And as the sun wheels down, his cloudy robes
Seem but a copy of the dyes of earth
Brought by his beams, to deck with fitting pomp
His passage from the glories he had seen
And smiled on, in his day-course through the sky.

November's storms have passed. The stern black frost
Blighting the pageant-leaves, has left them pale,
Shrunken, and sear; and the strong howling blasts
Have whirled them from their branches, darkening air,
And strewing them o'er earth. Now, sweet and calm,
Like music gliding o'er discordant sounds,
Or moonlight smiling on a troubled sea,
Summer, unrobed of all her glowing charms
That graced her prime, but mild and matron-like,
For a brief while returns to greet those scenes
O'er which she reigned in queenly loveliness.
A purple haze is trembling on the air,
Softening all near in veils of glimmering gauze,
And steeping far-off masses in thick mist
Blending their outlines with the shaded sky.
So still the atmosphere, the thistle's star
Drops motionless on the moss. Such quiet reigns,
The low, faint crackling of the dry fallen leaves
Stirred by the squirrel's foot is heard, and even
The light click of the milkweed's bursting pods,
Showing the glossy satin of the plumes
Close packed within, with which it wings its seeds.
The beech-nut falling from its opened burr,
Gives a sharp rattle; and the locust's song,

Rising and swelling shrill, then pausing short,
Rings like a trumpet. Distant woods and hills
Are full of echoes, and each sound that strikes
Upon the hollow air lets loose their tongues.
The ripples, creeping through the matted grass,
Drip on the ear, and the far partridge-drum
Rolls like low thunder. The last butterfly,
Like a winged violet, floating in the meek
Pink-colored sunshine, sinks his velvet feet
Within the pillared mullein's delicate down,
And shuts and opens his unruffled fans.
Lazily wings the crow with solemn croak
From tree-top, on to tree-top. Feebly chirps
The grasshopper, and the spider's tiny clock
Ticks from his crevice.
'T is the Sabbath-rest
Of Nature, ere she yields to Winter's power.

A softer breath is mingled with the keen
And piercing air, and o'er the frozen earth
And skeleton-forest, from the bleak northwest
Uplifts the storm-cloud, gathering fold on fold,
A rising mountain; o'er the sky it spreads,
A dull, impenetrable, gloomy gray.
The russet snow-bird twitters, as loose flakes,
One by one, float and flutter through the mist,
Spangling his wing and spotting where they light;
They thicken as they fall, until they stream
In myriad columns, mottling the dun air,
And drawing a dense screen around the sight;

The landscape whitens, and a shell-like sound
Murmurs, — the low-toned music of the snow.
Now roaring on its path, the chainless blast
Dashes in furious might, until the scene
Whirls one wild chaos; then exhausted sinks
With dying howls, its strength, and all is still.
The morning's sunshine glows upon a waste
Sparkling with diamonds. Bare the hill's steep brow,
But choked the hollow; meadow broad, and plain,
Are furrowed with white surges; fences stretch
Like low embankments, while the open woods
Are clothed in garbs of spotless purity.

Nature is Man's best teacher. She unfolds
Her treasures to his search, unseals his eye,
Illumes his mind, and purifies his heart.
An influence breathes from all the sights and sounds
Of her existence; she is Wisdom's self.
Rest yields she to the "weary" of the earth;
Its "heavy-laden" she endows with strength.
When sorrow presses on us, when the stings
Of bitter disappointment pierce our soul,
When our eye sickens at the sight of man,
Our ear turns loathing from his jarring voice,
The shadowy forest and the quiet field
Are then our comforters. A medicine
Breathes in the wind that fans our fevered brow,
The blessed sunshine yields a sweet delight,
The bird's low warble thrills within our breast,
The flower is eloquent with peace and joy,

And better thoughts come o'er us. Lighter heart
And purer feelings cheer our homeward way ;
We prize more deep the blessings that are ours,
And rest a higher, holier trust in God.

And when the splendid summer moonlight bathes,
Blinding the stars, Night's purple sky in rich
Transparent splendor, brightening all below,
As though earth's guardian angel watching o'er
Had dropped his silver mantle from his form
Upon her to protect her hêlpless sleep,
Nature speaks soothing music, stealing through
Each avenue to the heart, till all is peace :
Our thoughts are lifted, passions swept away,
And in our soul sweet holiness is shed ;
The feverish throbbings leave our brow, and sleep
Glides o'er our senses like a pleasant shade.

And Nature teaches us Philosophy :
In the quick shading of her brilliant morn
By the dark storm-cloud ; in the canker-spot
That lurks within her blushing fragrant rose,
In the sad blighting of her summer leaves
When Autumn wields his tempests ; solemnly
She warns how full of direst change is life ;
How perishing our sweetest, brightest joys ;
How oft death lays our dearest feelings waste,
And makes existence cold and desolate.
But oh ! she teaches also blessed Hope, —
Hope, the sustainer ! Hope, which keeps the heart

From breaking in its sorrow. Glorious Hope!
In the light seed that cradles the green plant,—
In the bright sun succeeding the dark night,—
In blue-eyed Spring, that plants her violets
Within departing Winter's melting snows.

And, holier theme, she teaches us of God,
Her Architect,—her Master. At His feet
She crouches, and in offering Him her praise
From myriad altars, and in myriad tones,
She bids man praise Him also. In the broad
Magnificent ocean surging in wild foam,
Yet bounded in its madness; in the fierce
Shrieking and howling tempest, crashing on
In desolating wrath, yet curbed with reins,
She shows His awful power, yet tender care;
In the free sunlight, in the dropping clouds,
And changes of the seasons, she proclaims
His boundless goodness, and exhaustless love.

Glorious, most glorious Nature! thus she yields
Gems to the seeker. But, alas! on earth
We see but dim reflections of her light,—
We hear but whispers of her magic voice.
Her dazzling, cloudless splendors will be seen,
And her full, perfect harmony be heard,
Only when, bursting from its chains of clay,
The soul shall reach its immortality.

ONNEKO.

Spring in the wilds! its crimson gems
    The gorgeous maple wore;
Rich satin tipped the beechen stems,
    The birch was tasselled o'er.
The wind-flower, first the bluebird sees,
When first he flits through budding trees,
    In myriads trembled round;
Soft from the south the air-breaths blew,
While every glowing sunbeam drew
    A violet from the ground.

The long rich rays of sunset fell
    Athwart the forest air,
And showed within a swampy dell,
    A form reclining there.
The scalp-lock o'er the brow, the cheeks
Fierce blazoned with the war-paint's streaks,
    The eye still keen and bold,
The totem on the bosom traced,
The wolf-robe twined around the waist,
    The Indian warrior told.

One hand still grasped the tomahawk,
    A broken gun lay near,

The last leaf of a withered stalk,
He came to perish here.
The thrasher, in the topmost tree
Whistled its varied harmony;
The redbird, fluttering by,
Seemed showering fire-sparks from its wings;
But naught to him these sounds and things,
His hour was come to die.

He marked the sunset radiance pour
Upon the field of fray,
Where, strewn like autumn leaves, in gore
His faithful warriors lay;
There, knife to bayonet, gun to gun,
Their blood in mingled streams had run;
Still, with their latest breath
Around their chieftain they had fought,
Yielding in stern despair to naught
But rapid slaughtering death.

And as he watched the gold and red
Along the western sky,
The visioned future pictured spread
To his prophetic eye.
Scattered and lost his race were driven,
Outcasts of earth and cursed by heaven,
With none to heed or save,
From scenes where once their fathers reigned,
To seek the refuge that remained
In far Pacific's wave.

The eve had deepened into night,
    The spangling star-gems now
Clustered around the moon, that bright
    Unveiled her silver brow ;
His winged thoughts sought the spot where free
And peacefully, and happily,
    He lived till white men came,
And turned, in midnight's stormiest gloom,
Where late were joy, and life, and bloom,
    To strife, and death, and flame.

Oh brightly rose that fancied scene
    Before the man of woe !
The waving forest's leafy screen,—
    The village roofs below;
The purple of the circling hills,
The diamond lake, the sparkling rills
    That veined the mountain side,
The dance, the chase, the fleet canoe,
His simple pomp, his warriors true,
    His tribesmen, and his bride.

But now a pall-like cloud was hung
    Around the blackened air,
And like a fiend the Tempest sprung
    From his sulphureous lair ;
In the fierce blast the pine-tree writhed,
Darted the lightning fiery scythed,
    The deafening thunder roared;
Roused from his den, the panther's shriek

Rung sharp, and clear, while from his peak
The frighted eagle soared.

Maddening, as wilder raged the night,
Thought burst its faint control,
Then swept the phantoms of the fight
Across the Sachem's soul;
Once more he whirled his hatchet high,
Once more he whooped his battle-cry,
As, staggering mid his foes,
Plume, knife, and bosom raining blood,
He for an instant sternly stood,
And sank beneath their blows.

Just then, broad, bright, and blinding, flashed
The lightning o'er the gloom;
And down, bare, scorched, and sppintered, dashed
A cedar's kingly plume;
The cloud, the earth, the trunks, the sprays,
Within that blue and sheeted blaze,
Leaped startling into light:
It passed; but in that fiery car,
The Sachem's soul had swept afar
In its returnless flight.

The frequent gleams of sunny gold,
The pleasant showers of rain,
And warmth pervading Nature, told
That spring had come again;
The leaf-buds swelled upon the bough,

A soft mist clothed the mountain's brow,
And sweetly from the hill
The bluebird's mirthful carol blent
With flute-like, murmuring voices sent
From many a snow-born rill.

In a wild, lurking gorge that wound
Amid the mountain shade,
Lost in the mazes of their ground,
A group of hunters strayed;
The weighty rifle, pouch, and horn,
Alike by youth and age were borne,
For toil their limbs had strung;
And woods, whose years were centuries,
Had melted like the passing breeze,
Where'er their axes rung.

Oft did they seek that passage dark
To pierce with practised sight,
Oft scan the moss upon the bark
To guide their footsteps right;
From the dead leaves young grass-blades peered,
Its downy curl the fern upreared,
Fresh fringe the hemlock showed;
The blossomed shadbush crouching low,
Scattered its frequent patch of snow
Along their tangled road.

From the twined root the partridge whirred,
The striped snake sought its den,

Shrill chirped the squirrel, as were heard
Strange voices in the glen;
Filling the woods with fleeting roar,
The startled pigeon flock whizzed o'er,
The robin called in fright;
And once the branches near them crashed,
And the fierce wild-cat screaming dashed
Before in leaping flight.

At length the misty atmosphere
Breathed pestilent and damp,
And laurels clustering thick and drear,
Proclaimed the sunken swamp;
Black straggling trees, with long gray moss
And rotting bark, like ghosts across
The waste, their branches spread;
A melancholy stillness reigned
Around, as if there naught remained
But relics of the dead.

A thicket, denser than the rest,
Along their wayside grew,
They plunge within its net-like breast—
Ha! what is that they view?
There lay a grinning skeleton,
Where scarce could pierce the summer sun
Or breathe the summer air;
Some helpless dweller of the woods
Starving, amidst these solitudes,
Had doubtless perished there.

The creeping ground-pine twined about
Each shrunk and fleshless limb,
And the white wind-flower looked from out
The sockets black and grim;
Half-hidden in the foliage round,
With which spring clothes the forest ground
In blossom, leaf, and stalk,
Reddened with rust, there lay upon
The moss, the fragment of a gun,
And dinted tomahawk.

One with white hair, then kneeling low,
The tomahawk swept bare,
And read the letters "Onneko"
In rude marked traces there;
The memory of a forest King
Was brought on Thought's recurring wing
From twilight of the past,
Who, scorning fierce to bend the knee,
For vengeance and for liberty
Long strove, but fell at last.

The old man told his story then,
How in a distant wood,
Embosomed in a pleasant glen,
An Indian village stood.
There was the lake, whose blue expanse
Pictured the council, and the dance,—
The pirogue's simple sail, —
And war-post, where for Onneko

A hundred warriors struck the blow,
And rushed upon the trail.

Then, how the white men sought the lake,
Like vultures for their prey,
With craft and worthless toys to take
Those hunting-grounds away;
How baffled: one wild night of dread,
The black sky gleamed with lurid red
From burning roofs, and loud
The Sachem heard the musket crash,
And saw the blood-stained bayonet flash,
From out the sulphurous shroud.

Then how those smouldering heaps among
That prophesied his fate,
The maddened chief his death-song sung,
And swore eternal hate;
In wolf-trod swamps, and mountains where
The lurking panther made his lair,
The noble savage fought;
There oft his war-whoop startling rose,
Till borne down by unnumbered foes,
He died the death he sought.

Then through the listening group, a grief
Weighty and deep was spread,
They with one impulse raised the chief.
From that damp thicket's bed.
They delved a grave within the sod,

While to the Indian's Christian's God
    The old man poured his prayer,
Beneath a hemlock's mournful shade,
The relics of the Sachem laid,
    And left him resting there.

A FOREST NOOK.

A NOOK within the forest: overhead
The branches arch, and shape a pleasant bower,
Breaking white cloud, blue sky, and sunshine bright,
Into pure ivory and sapphire spots,
And flecks of gold; a soft, cool, emerald tint
Colors the air, as though the delicate leaves
Emitted self-born light. What splendid walls,
And what a gorgeous roof carved by the hand
Of cunning Nature! Here the spruce thrusts in
Its bristling plume, tipped with its pale-green points;
The scalloped beech-leaf, and the birch's cut
Into fine ragged edges, interlace.
While here and there, through clefts, the laurel lifts
Its snowy chalices half-brimmed with dew,
As though to hoard it for the haunting elves
The moonlight calls to this their festal hall.
A thick, rich, grassy carpet clothes the earth,
Sprinkled with autumn leaves. The fern displays
Its fluted wreath, beaded beneath with drops
Of richest brown; the wild-rose spreads its breast
Of delicate pink, and the o'erhanging fir
Has dropped its dark, long cone.
                                        The scorching glare
Without, makes this green nest a grateful haunt

For summer's radiant things: the butterfly
Fluttering within and resting on some flower,
Fans his rich velvet form; the toiling bee
Shoots by, with sounding hum and mist-like wings;
The robin perches on the bending spray
With shrill, quick chirp; and like a flake of fire
The redbird seeks the shelter of the leaves.
And now and then a flutter overhead
In the thick green, betrays some wandering wing
Coming and going, yet concealed from sight.
A shrill, loud outcry, — on yon highest bough
Sits the gray squirrel, in his burlesque wrath
Stamping and chattering fiercely: now he drops
A hoarded nut, then at my smiling gaze
Buries himself within the foliage.
The insect tribe are here: the ant toils on
With its white burden; in its netted web,
Gray glistening o'er the bush, the spider lurks,
A close-crouched ball, out-darting as a hum
Tells its trapped prey, and looping quick its threads,
Chains into helplessness the buzzing wings.
The wood-tick taps its tiny muffled drum
To the shrill cricket-fife, and, swelling loud,
The grasshopper its swelling bugle winds.
Those breaths of Nature, the light fluttering airs
Like gentle respirations, come and go,
Lift on its crimson stem the maple leaf,
Displaying its white lining underneath,
And sprinkle from the tree-tops golden rain
Of sunshine on the velvet sward below.

Such nooks as this are common in the woods:
And all these sights and sounds the commonest
In Nature when she wears her summer prime.
Yet by them pass not lightly; to the wise
They tell the beauty and the harmony
Of even the lowliest things that God hath made.
That His familiar earth and sky are full
Of His ineffable power and majesty;
That in the humble objects, seen too oft
To be regarded, shines such wondrous grace,
The art of man is vain to imitate;
That the low flower our careless foot treads down
Stands a rich shrine of incense delicate,
And radiant beauty; and that God hath formed
All, from the cloud-wreathed mountain, to the grain
Of silver sand the bubbling spring casts up,
With deepest forethought and severest care.
And thus these noteless, lovely things are types
Of His perfection and divinity.

THE WILLEWEMOC IN SUMMER.

BUBBLING within some basin green
  So fringed with fern, the woodcock's bill
Scarce penetrates the leafy screen,
  Leaps into life the infant rill.
Oozing along, a winding streak,
O'er moss and grass, it whispers meek,
Then swelling o'er some barrier root
The tiny ripples onward shoot,
Then the clear sparkling waters spread
And deepen down their sloping bed,
Until, a streamlet bright and strong,
The Willewemoc glides along
Through its wild forest depths, to bear
Its homage to the Delaware.

Now pebbly shallows, where the deer
  Just bathes his crossing hoof, and now
Broad hollowed creeks, that, deep and clear,
  Would whelm him to his antlered brow.
Here, the smooth silver sleeps so still,
The ear might catch the faintest trill;
The bee's low hum, the whirr of wings,
And the sweet songs of grass-hid things.

There, dashing by, in booming shocks,
  So loud their wrath the waters wreak,
Mid floating trees and scattered rocks,
  They drown the fierce gray eagle's shriek.
Here, the slight cowslip from the moss
In ripples breaks the amber gloss;
There, the whirled spray showers upward fly
To the slant firs crag-rooted high.

Blue sky, pearl cloud, and golden beam
  Beguile my steps this summer day,
Beside the lone and lovely stream,
  And through its sylvan scenes to stray:
The moss, too delicate and soft
To bear the tripping bird aloft,
Slopes its green velvet to the sedge,
Tufting the mirrored water's edge,
Where the slow eddies wrinkling creep
Mid swaying grass in stillness deep:
The sweet wind scarce has breath to turn
  The edges of the leaves, or stir
  The fragile wreath of gossamer
Embroidered on yon clump of fern.
The stream incessant greets my ear
  In hollow dashings, full round tones,
Purling through alder branches here,
  There gurgling o'er the tinkling stones;
The rumble of the waterfall,
Majestic sounding over all.

Before me spreads the sheltered pool,
Pictured with tree-shapes black and cool;
Here, the roofed water seems to be
A solid mass of ebony;
There, the broad surface glances bright
In dazzling gleams of spangled light;
Now the quick darting waterfly
Ploughs its light furrow, skimming by,
While circling o'er in mazy rings,
The chirping swallow dips his wings;
Relieved against yon sunny glare
The gnat-swarms, dust-like, speck the air;
From yon deep cove where lily-gems
Are floating by their silken stems,
Out glides the dipping duck, to seek
The narrow windings of the creek,
The glitterings of his purple back
Disclosing far his sinuous track;
Now, sliding down yon grassy brink
I see the otter plunge and sink,
Yon bubbling streak betrays his rise,
And through the furrowing sheet he plies.

The aspen shakes, the hemlock hums,
Damp with the shower the west wind comes;
Rustling in heaps the quivering grass,
It darkening dots the streamlet's glass,
And rises with the herald-breeze
The cloud's dark umber o'er the trees;
A veil of gauze-like mist it flings,

Dimples the stream with transient rings,
And soon beneath this tent-like tree
The swift, bright glancing streaks I see,
And hear around in murmuring strain
The gentle music of the rain.
Then bursts the sunshine warm and gay,
The misty curtain melts away,
The cloud in fragments breaks, and through
Trembles in spots the smiling blue;
A fresh, damp sweetness fills the scene,
  From dripping leaf and moistened earth,
The odor of the winter-green,
  Floats on the airs that now have birth;
Dashes and air-bells all about
Proclaim the gambols of the trout,
And calling bush and answering tree
Echo with woodland melody.
Now the piled west in pomp displays
  The radiant forms that sunset weaves;
And slanting lines of golden haze
  Are streaming through the sparkling leaves.
A clear, sweet, joyous strain is heard, —
It is the minstrel mocking-bird.
The strain of every songster floats
Within his rich and splendid notes;
The bluebird's warble, brief and shrill;
The wailing of the whippoorwill;
The robin's call, the jay's harsh screech,
His own sweet music heard through each.
His three-toned anthem now he sings,

Liquid and low and soft it rings;
Then rising with a swell more clear,
It melts upon the bending ear,
Till with a piercing flourished flight,
He bids the darkening scene good-night.

THE CALLICOON IN AUTUMN.

FAR in the forest's heart, unknown,
  Except to sun and breeze,
Where solitude her dreaming throne
  Has held for centuries;
Chronicled by the rings and moss
That tell the flight of years across
  The seamed and columned trees,
This lovely streamlet glides along
With tribute of eternal song!

Now, stealing through its thickets deep
  In which the wood-duck hides;
Now, picturing in its basin sleep
  Its green, pool-hollow'd sides;
Here, through the pebbles slow it creeps,
There, in some wild abyss it sweeps,
  And foaming, hoarsely chides;
Then slides so still, its gentle swell
Scarce ripples round the lily's bell.

Nature, in her autumnal dress
  Magnificent and gay,

Displays her brightest loveliness,
  Though nearest her decay;
The sky is spread in silvery sheen,
With breaks of tenderest blue between,
  Through which the timid ray
Struggles in faintest, meekest glow,
And rests in dreamy hues below.

The southwest airs of ladened balm
  Come breathing sweetly by,
And wake, amid the forest's calm,
  One quick and shivering sigh,
Shaking, but dimpling not the glass
Of this smooth streamlet, as they pass,
  They scarcely wheel on high
The thistle's downy, silver star,
To waft its pendent seed afar.

Sleep-like the silence, by the lapse
  Of waters only broke,
And the woodpecker's fitful taps
  Upon the hollow oak;
And, mingling with the insect hum,
The beatings of the partridge drum,
  With now and then a croak,
As, on his flapping wing, the crow
O'er passes, heavily and slow.

A foliage world of glittering dyes
  Gleams brightly on the air,

As though a thousand sunset skies,
  With rainbows, blended there;
Each leaf an opal, and each tree
A bower of varied brilliancy,
  And all one general glare
Of splendor that o'erwhelms the sight
With dazzling and unequalled light.

Rich gold with gorgeous crimson, here,
  The birch and maple twine,
The beech its orange mingles near
  With emerald of the pine;
And even the humble bush and herb
Are glowing with those tints superb,
  As though a scattered mine
Of gems upon the earth were strown,
Flashing with radiance, each its own.

All steeped in that delicious charm
  Peculiar to our land,
That comes, ere Winter's frosty arm
  Knits Nature's icy band;
The purple, rich, and glimmering smoke,
That forms the Indian Summer's cloak,
  When, by soft breezes fanned,
For a few precious days he broods
Amid the gladdened fields and woods.

The squirrel chatters merrily,
  The nut falls ripe and brown,

And, gem-like, from the jewelled tree
  The leaf comes fluttering down;
And restless in his plumage gay,
From bush to bush loud screams the jay,
  And on the hemlock's crown
The sentry pigeon guards from foe
The flock that dots the woods below.

See! on this edge of forest lawn,
  Where sleeps the clouded beam,
A doe has led her spotted fawn
  To gambol by the stream;
Beside yon mullein's braided stalk
They hear the gurgling voices talk,
  While, like a wandering gleam,
The yellow-bird dives here and there,
A feathered vessel of the air.

On, through the rampart walls of rock,
  The waters pitch in white,
And high, in mist, the cedars lock
  Their boughs, half lost to sight
Above the whirling gulf, — the dash
Of frenzied floods, that vainly lash
  Their limits in their flight,
Whose roar the eagle, from his peak,
Responds to with his angriest shriek.

Stream of the wilds! the Indian here,
  Free as thy chainless flow,

Has bent against thy depths his spear,
  And in thy woods his bow, —
The beaver built his dome ; but they,
The memories of an earlier day, —
  Like those dead trunks, that show
What once were mighty pines, — have fled
With Time's unceasing, rapid tread.

THE HILL HOLLOW.

A HOLLOW in the hills. Spring's melted snows
And many rain-showers swelled the tiny brook,
Until it dashed a torrent, scooping out
A channel, as it tore upon its way.
But now, the slender springlet trickles on,
Purling and murmuring, with so low a voice
The whizzing of yon humming-bird's swift wings,
Spanning gray glimmering circles round its shape,
Is heard above the prattle. Green and sweet
And quiet lies the hollow. From the road,
Furrowed with wheels, and beaten hard with feet,
A few short steps will place you in the depth
Of this soft lap of Nature. When the sun
Quivers upon the dust, and on the brow
Burns hot and fierce, and short the panting breath,
With what refreshing coolness does the air
Moisten your lips, and glide around your limbs,
Strengthening again to vigor ! High o'erhead
The yellow bank, scarped by the rushing flood,
Dangling with threads of roots, with here and there
The twisted feet of clinging firs, like veins
Bare, bulging from the earth, and bedded stones,
And crowned with ranks of tall, majestic trees,

Casts a black massive shadow half across.
The short, thick emerald grass slopes opposite,
In a tall graceful curve, to where the rill
Glides in its sparkling dance, with castanets
Made by the pebble tricklings.

August noon
Brightens the blue, and sunshine bathes with gold
The slope before me. In the faint light airs
The aspen shakes with laughter, but the pine
Scarce moves a tassel, and the maple turns
The pale green backs of its broad scalloped leaves
Lazily over. All around I scent
The breath of ripening things ; the clustered grape,
The apple of the thorn, the mandrake's fruit,
Looking like lemons either side its stem,
And the low everlasting's fragrance rich,
O'erpowering all, when near its satin leaves.
The mullein's pillar, tipped with golden flowers,
Slim rises upward, and yon yellow-bird
Shoots to its top ; a crested jay has made
That jointed rush a pedestal, and couched
Within this thistle's tuft are three bright bees.
A fox's den gapes, shelving, by yon root,
Thick clustered o'er with shrubs ; and this light track
Tells where the kine come winding down to drink.
Lovely the scene, yet is it but a line
In Nature's teeming volume, free to all
Who seek to read it ; strange that men will not,
When its bright leaves are scatter'd round their path

Like many a blessing also is the scene,
Lurking beside the track on which we move
In all our dim pursuits ; and only hid
By some slight veiling screen of circumstance,
Because we lack the knowledge, or are loth
To make the effort that would gain the prize.
Knowledge will come with seeking ; circumstance
Will fall before the effort, and the cool
Green beauty of the blessing, when the brow
Burns with the feverish strugglings of the world,
And heart and limb are weary in the war —
The wolfish war of man with fellow-man, —
For might, or gold, or glory will be ours.

MIDSUMMER.

An August day! a dreamy haze
  Films air, and mingles with the skies
Sweetly the rich, dark sunshine plays,
  Bronzing each object where it lies.
Outlines are melted in the gauze
  That Nature veils; the fitful breeze
From the thick pine, low murmuring draws;
  Then dies in flutterings through the trees.
The bee is slumbering in the thistle,
And, now and then, a broken whistle —
A tread — a hum — a tap — is heard
  Through the dry leaves, in grass and bush,
As insect, animal, and bird
  Rouse, brief from their lethargic hush.
Then, even these pleasant sounds would cease,
  And a dead stillness all things lock,
  The aspen seem like sculptured rock,
  And not a tassel-thread be shaken
  The monarch-pine's deep trance to waken,
And Nature settle prone in drowsy peace.
The misty blue, — the distant masses, —
  The air, in woven purple glimmering, —
The shiver transiently that passes

Over the leaves, as though each tree
  Gave one brief sigh, — the slumberous shimmering
  Of the red light, — invested seem
    With some sweet charm, that soft, serene,
    Mellows the gold — the blue — the green
Into mild-tempered harmony,
    And melts the sounds that intervene,
  As scarce to break the quiet, till we deem
Nature herself transformed to Fancy's dream.

OSCEOLA.

PART I.

THE rich blue sky is o'er,
  Around are the tall green trees,
And the jessamine's breath from the everglade
  Is borne on the wandering breeze.
On the mingled grass and flowers
  Stands a fierce and threatening form,
That looks like an eagle when pluming his wing
  To brave the gathering storm.

His rifle within his grasp, —
  The bright plume o'er his head, —
His features are clothed with a warrior's pride,
  And he moves with a monarch's tread.
He bends his listening ear,
  He peers through the tangled screen,
And he smiles with joy, as the flash of steel
  Through the everglade's grass is seen.

One wave of his stalwart arm,
  Wild forms around him stand,

And his eye glares bright with triumphant light
  As he looks at his swarthy band.
At the hammock's flowery edge
  Nearer the bayonet's glow
The pale-face ranks are rallying,
  But they seek in vain the foe.

They see in that lovely scene
  But the humming-bird o'er the flowers,
And the glittering wing of the paroquet
  In the cool and fragrant bowers.
But hark! from the cypress shade,
  From the bay-tree's glossy leaves,
And the nooks where the vine from bough to bough
  Its serpent-like festoon weaves,

The loud, shrill warwhoops burst
  On the soft and sleeping air,
And the quick, bright darts of surrounding death
  Are fearfully glancing there.
The eagle with fierce delight
  Abroad has his pinion cast,
And he shrieks as he bathes in the crimson rain,
  And sweeps through the whizzing blast.

The battle-storm is o'er, —
  The hammock is reeking red, —
But who looks there with victorious smile
  On the heaps of the pale-face dead?

'T is a tribe's young warrior-chief!
  The deeds of whose vengeful flame
Have filled the ear of a mighty land
  With the terror of his name.

He leaps from his covert dark
  Like the fire-flash from the smoke,
And the hamlet awakes from its midnight sleep
  At his tomahawk's lightning stroke.
He enters the peaceful cot,
  And more blood-drops there he leaves
Than the multiflora's crimson gems
  That are trailed about the eaves.

PART II.

In a dark and dungeon room
  Is stretched a tawny form,
And it shakes in its dreadful agony
  Like a leaf in the autumn storm.
No pillared palmetto hangs
  Its tuft in the clear, bright air,
But a sorrowing group, and the narrow wall,
  And a smouldering hearth are there.

The white froth on his lip,
  His trembling, gasping breath,
And the hollow rattle in his throat
  Proclaim the conqueror, death.

'T is the proud, victorious chief
  Who smiled mid the pale-face slain ;
'T is the eagle that swept through the whizzing blast
  And bathed in the crimson rain.

For his own green forest home
  He had struggled long and well,
But the soul that had breasted a nation's arms
  At the touch of a fetter, fell.
He had worn wild freedom's crown
  On his bright unconquered brow
Since he first saw the light of his beautiful skies :
  It was gone forever now !

But still in his last dread hour
  Did not bright visions bloom ?
Bright visions that shed a golden gleam
  On the darkness of his doom :
They calmed his throbbing pulse,
  And they hung on his muttering breath :
The spray thrown up from life's frenzied flood
  Plunging on to the gulf of death.

The close walls shrunk away ;
  Above was the stainless sky,
And the lakes, with their floating isles of flowers,
  Spread glittering to his eye.
O'er his hut, the live-oak spread
  Its branching, gigantic shade, —

With its dots of leaves and its robes of moss
  Broad blackening on the glade.

But a sterner sight rolls round:
  Battle's wild torrent is there,
The tomahawk gleams, and the red blood streams,
  And the warwhoops rend the air.
At the head of his faithful band
  He peals forth his terrible cry,
As he fiercely leaps mid the slaughtered heaps
  Of the foe that but fought to die.

* * * * * * * * *

One gasp : and the eye is glazed,
  And still is the stiffening clay;
The eagle soul of the chief had passed
  On the battle's flood away.

THE SCHOOL-HOUSE.

In a green lane that from the village street
Diverges, stands the school-house ; long and low
The frame, and blackened with the hues of Time.
Around it spreads the green with scattered trees ;
Fenced fields and orchards stretching either hand,
And fronting. When the strawberry ripe and red
Is nestling at the roots of the deep grass,
And when the autumn sun has decked with gold
And crimson the gnarled apple-bough, light paths
Stretch from the play-ground, worn by urchin feet,
To the forbidden treasures ; forays sad !
For fingers stained, or bulging pockets oft
Betrayed what the faint sobbing voice denied.
A picture of soft beauty shines the scene
When painted by the sinking summer sun
In tints of light and shade ; but winter's gloom
Shows nothing but a waste, with one broad track
Stamped to the humble door-post from the lane ;
The snow-capped wood-pile stretching near the walls ;
And the half-severed log with axe that leans
Within the gaping notch.

The room displays
Long rows of desk and bench ; the former stained

And streaked with blots and trickles of dried ink,
Lumbered with maps and slates and well-thumbed
books,
And carved with rude initials ; while the knife
Has hacked and sliced the latter. In the midst
Stands the dread throne whence breathes supreme
command,
And in a locked recess well known, is laid
The dread regalia, gifted with a charm
Potent to the rebellious. When the bell
Tinkles the school-hour, inward streams the crowd,
And bending heads proclaim the task begun.
Upon his throne, with magisterial brow,
The teacher sits, round casting frowning looks
As the low giggle and the shuffling foot
Betray the covert jest, or idleness.
Oft does he call, with deep and pompous voice,
The class before him; and shrill, chattering tones
In pert or blundering answers, break the soft
And dreamy hum of study, heretofore
Like beehive sounds prevailing. Now, perchance,
Some luckless urchin stands before the throne,
With features swoln as scarce to keep the tears,
And shoulders raised, while the detected fault
Is forth paraded, and the broken law
Learnedly dwelt on: then with staring sight,
Face all awry, and chattering teeth, he sees
The sceptre taken slowly from its nook,
A whip with thongs: pursues with blinking gaze
Its upward motion, then, with hideous yell,
Tells that the whizzing blow falls not in vain.

Now rising from his seat, the teacher strides
Athwart the room; as treads he past, each desk
Starts into industry: white figures grow
Upon the slate; black, spattering pothooks sprawl
Upon the blotted, dog-eared copy-book;
And eyes are glued upon the letters huge
And pictures of the primer: as he wheels,
The wandering glance has scarcely time to sink,
The queer grimace, and the replying grin
To vanish; each regaining its mute sway
As turns the back upon them. But bright noon
Now through the casement streams in quivering haze,
And gushes on the floor: the word is given,
And, bursting from the thraldom, rush without
The merry throngs, and breaking into groups,
Drive their loud pastime on the sunny green.
Here flies the ball, — there shoots the marble, — now
The racers seek the goal, — each sinew now
Is straining in the leap, — while heartfelt mirth
Echoes upon the soft and balmy air:
The clouds that float and wreathe upon the breeze
Not more restrainless than those happy hearts.
The glee, bright contrast to the sullen looks
And lingering steps with which each urchin seeks,
At the sad summons of the morning bell,
The hated porch. Yet is the school-house rude,
As is the chrysalis to the butterfly,
To the rich flower the seed. The dusky walls
Hold the fair germs of knowledge; and the tree,
Glorious in beauty, golden with its fruits,
To the low school-house traces back its life.

THE MINISINK.

ENCIRCLED by the screening shade,
  With scattered bush, and bough,
And grassy slopes, a pleasant glade
  Lies spread before me now;
The wind, that shows its forest search
By the sweet fragrance of the birch,
  Is whispering on my brow,
And the mild sunshine flickers through
The soft white cloud and summer blue.

Far to the North, the Delaware
  Flows, mountain-curved, along,
By forest bank, by summit bare,
  It bends in rippling song;
Receiving in each eddying nook
The waters of the vassal brook,
  It sweeps more deep and strong;
Round yon green island it divides,
And by this quiet woodland glides.

The ground-bird flutters from the grass
  That hides her tiny nest;
The startled deer, as by I pass,
  Bounds in the thicket's breast;

The redbird rears his crimson wing
From the long fern of yonder spring:
  A sweet and peaceful rest
Breathes o'er the scene, where once the sound
Of battle shook the gory ground.

Long will the shuddering hunter tell
  How once red warriors rose,
And wakened with their battle-yell
  The forest's long repose.
How shrieked in vain babe, wife, and sire,
As hatchet, scalping-knife, and fire,
  Proclaimed their bloody foes;
Until the boldest quailed to mark,
Wrapped round the woods, Night's mantle dark.

At length the fisher furled his sail
  Within the sheltered creek,
The hunter trod his forest trail
  The mustering band to seek;
The settler cast his axe away,
And grasped his rifle for the fray:
  All came, revenge to wreak,
With the rude arms that chance supplied,—
And die, or conquer, side by side.

Behind the footsteps of their foe
  They rushed, a gallant throng,
Burning with haste to strike a blow
  For each remembered wrong;

Here on this field of Minisink,
Fainting they sought the river's brink,
  Where cool waves gushed along;
No sound within the woods they heard,
But murmuring wind and warbling bird.

A scream!—'t is but the panther's; naught
  Breaks the calm sunshine there;
A thicket stirs! — a deer has sought
  From sight a closer lair;
Again upon the grass they droop,
When burst close round, the well-known whoop,
  Shrill, deafening on the air;
And onward from their ambush deep,
Like wolves the savage warriors leap.

In vain upsprung that gallant band
  And seized their weapons by,
Fought eye to eye, and hand to hand,
  Alas! 't was but to die;
In vain the rifle's deadly flash
Scorched eagle plume and wampum sash;
  The hatchet hissed on high,
And down they fell in crimson heaps,
Like the ripe corn the sickle reaps.

In vain they sought the covert dark;
  The knife gashed every head,
Each arrow found unerring mark,
  Till earth was piled with dead.

Oh ! long the matron watched to hear
Loved tones and footsteps meet her ear,
  Till hope grew faint with dread.
Long did she search the wood-paths o'er, —
Those tones and steps she heard no more.

Years have passed by, the merry bee
  Hums round the laurel flowers,
The mock-bird pours its melody
  Amid the forest bowers ;
A skull is at my feet, though now
The wild rose wreathes its bony brow,
  Relic of other hours, —
It bids the wandering pilgrim think
Of those who died at Minisink.

A SEPTEMBER STROLL.

THE dull mist of September, fitfully
Thickening to chill and gusty streams of rain,
Lifted at sunset, and the western verge
Showed a broad stripe of light; a golden smile
Burst o'er the dripping scene, then died away:
And the North swept, in hollow moan and hiss,
Round dwellings and through branches.
Morning broke
In cloudless beauty, but a chilly breath
Still edged the crystal air. The sun went down,
With a rich halo glowing round the spot
Where his orb glided, and a splendid belt
Of orange burned above his slanting track,
Melting to soft, bright gray, that deepened up
Into the rich mid-blue; and where the pearl
Darkened into the sapphire, bounded forth
The courier-star of night's magnificence.
Morning again rose gloriously clear:
The air was softer, and the gentle West
Went fanning where the North had struck its chill;
And as the sun climbed up, his light was cast
So warm and genial, and the atmosphere
Was felt so sweetly and deliciously,

It seemed 't were pleasure merely to lie down,
And bask and breathe.
The noontide now has come:
Green woods and pleasant fields are smiling forth
Inviting welcome. Let us leave the walls
Of the close city, and with wandering feet
Seek the sweet haunts of Nature. O'er the dust
Of the great thoroughfare, with rapid wheels
And trampling hoofs vexed ever, where the gay
And flaunting motes sport thick in Fashion's beam,
Idle and worthless, quick we tread, and turn
Gladly aside, where a green, narrow lane
Leads to a wild ravine amid the hills.
Smooth fields, with browsing cattle, are around,
And now and then the tinkling sheep-bell breaks
Pleasantly on the ear. Our pathway leads
Through a rude gate and o'er a broken bridge,
Where the green rushes and long tangled grass
Proclaim the shrunken streamlet; a faint track
Leads to a barrelled spring, whose waters boil
Unceasing from their loose, gray sandy depth.
Grass spreads its sides with velvet, and tall trees
Drop their black shapes around. We pass along:
A gorge winds up, walled in with rocky banks
Plumaged with leaning branches; wheel-marks deep
Are traced upon the stone floor of the chasm,
And grateful shadow rests like sleep within.
Grim roots start out from crevices; green sprouts
Flaunt from mossed ledges; and large trickling drops,
From the steep sides, shed moisture on the air.

We rest awhile, then tread again our path.
A grassy glade, with points and curving banks,
The dry bed of a streamlet, lures our steps.
The varied aster tribes stand clustered round;
The gnarled thorn shows its yellow-crimson fruit,
Studding its boughs, and scattered thick beneath ;
And from the brinks the solidago bends
Its golden feather: mingling with the sweet
And peaceful quiet, low monotonous sounds
Stream from the insects, varied with the swell
Of the near locust's peevish clarion,
And chirping of the cricket. Now the fence
We leap, and stray into the broad green field.
The air is an elixir; as we breathe,
The blood swift tingles in our veins; we long
To bound with transport and shout out our joy.
The thread-like gossamer is waving past,
Borne on the wind's light wing, and to yon branch,
Tangled and trembling, clings like snowy silk.
The thistle-down, high lifted through the rich
Bright blue, quick float, like gliding stars, and then
Touching the sunshine, flash, and seem to melt
Within the dazzling brilliance. Yon tall oak,
Standing from out the straggling skirt of wood,
Touched by the frost, that wondrous chemist, shows
Spottings of gorgeous crimson through its green,
Like a proud monarch, towering still erect,
Though sprinkled with his life-blood. Close beside,
That aspen, to the wind's soft-fingered touch,
Flutters with all its dangling leaves, as though

Beating with myriad pulses. Misty shade
Films the deep hollows, misty sunshine glows
On the round hills. Across the far-off wood,
The atmosphere is shaded like thin smoke,
Until we fancy a dim swarm of motes
Is glimmering there and dancing. We approach,
And tread the dark recesses: withered leaves
Spread a thick, crackling mantle; countless trunks
Lead on the eye in labyrinths, till lost
Within a dizzy maze, and overhead
A vast and interlacing roof of green.
The hickory-shell, cracked open by its fall,
Shows its ripe fruit, an ivory ball, within;
And the cleft chestnut-burr displays its sheath
White glistening, with its glossy nuts below.
Scattered around, the wild rose-bushes hang,
Their ruby buds tipping their thorny sprays.
The everlasting's blossoms seem as cut
In delicate silver, whitening o'er the slopes;
The seedy clematis, branched high, is robed
With woolly tufts; the snowy Indian-pipe
Is streaked with black decay; the wintergreen
Offers its berries; and the prince's-pine,
Scarce seen above the fallen leaves, peers out,
A firm, green, glossy wreath.

Within this knot
Of twining roots, a shelving aperture
Proclaims the hedgehog's chamber; through the gloom
Within we see the sparkle of his eye,

And his slim snout thrust level with the brink
To scent his danger ; but fear not ! no staff
Will pierce thy winding cavern, to drive forth
Thy crouching form, and beat, with cruel blows,
Thy gasping being from thee.
By we pass,
And from the darkening woods released, we see
One mass of shadow stretching to the east,
And narrow stripes of gold upon the tops
Of hill and tree ; and climbing the ascent,
We view the sun sink calmly to his rest.

WHITE LAKE.[1]

PURE as their parent springs! how bright
  The silvery waters stretch away,
Reposing in the pleasant light
  Of June's most lovely day.

Curving around the eastern side,
  Rich meadows slope their banks, to meet,
With fringe of grass and fern, the tide
  Which sparkles at their feet.

Here, busy life attests that toil,
  With its quick talisman, has made
Fields green and waving, from a soil
  Of rude and savage shade.

While opposite, the forest lies
  In giant shadow, black and deep,
Filling with leaves the circling sky,
  And frowning in its sleep.

1 Or "Lake Kau-na-ong-ga," meaning literally "*two wings.*" White Lake, which is the unmeaning modern epithet of this beautiful sheet of water, is situated in the town of Bethel, Sullivan county, N. Y. It is in the form of a pair of huge wings expanded.

Amid this scene of light and gloom,
  Nature with art links hand in hand,
Thick woods beside soft rural bloom,
  As by a seer's command.

Here, waves the grain ; here, curls the smoke ;
  The orchard bends ; there, wilds, as dark
As when the hermit waters woke
  Beneath the Indian's bark.

Oft will the panther's startling shriek
  With the herd's quiet lowings swell,
The wolf's fierce howl terrific break
  Upon the sheepfold's bell.

The ploughman sees the wind-winged deer
  Dart from his covert to the wave,
And fearless in its mirror clear
  His branching antlers lave.

Here, the green headlands seem to meet
  So near, a fairy bridge might cross ;
There, spreads the broad and limpid sheet
  In smooth, unruffled gloss.

Arched by the thicket's screening leaves,
  A lilied harbor lurks below,
Where on the sand each ripple weaves
  Its melting wreath of snow.

Hark ! like an organ's tones, the woods
  To the light wind in murmurs wake,
The voice of the vast solitudes
  Is speaking to the lake.

The fanning air-breath sweeps across
  On its broad path of sparkles now,
Bends down the violet to the moss,
  Then melts upon my brow.

AN AMERICAN SPRING.

Now fluttering breeze, now stormy blast,
  Mild rain, then blustering snow :
Winter's stern, fettering cold is past,
  But where Spring's genial glow ?
The white cloud floats in smiling blue,
The broad, bright sunshine's golden hue
  Bathes the still frozen earth :
A change ! above, black vapors roll ;
We turn from our expected stroll,
  And seek the blazing hearth.

Hark ! that sweet carol ! what delight !
  The scene no more is dumb.
The little bluebird greets our sight, —
  Spring, magic Spring, has come !
The south wind's kiss is on the air,
The melting snow-wreaths everywhere
  Are leaping off in showers ;
And Nature, in her brightening looks,
Tells that her flowers, and leaves, and brooks,
  And birds will soon be ours.

A few soft, sunny days are here,
  The air has lost its chill,
A bright, green tinge succeeds the sear
  Upon the southern hill.
Off to the woods! a pleasant scene!
Here sprouts the fresh young wintergreen,
  There swells a mossy mound;
Though in the hollows drifts are piled,
The wandering wind is sweet and mild,
  And buds are bursting round.

Where its long rings unwinds the fern,
  The violet, nestling low,
Casts back the white lid of its urn,
  Its purple streaks to show:
Beautiful blossom! first to rise
And smile beneath Spring's wakening skies,
  The courier of the band
Of coming flowers, what feelings sweet
Flow, as the silvery gem we meet
  Upon its needle-wand.

A sudden roar, — a shade is cast, —
  We look up with a start,
And, sounding like a transient blast,
  O'erhead the pigeons dart;
Scarce their blue glancing shapes the eye
Can trace, ere, dotted on the sky,
  They wheel in distant flight.
A chirp! and swift the squirrel scours

Along the prostrate trunk, and cowers
  Within its clefts from sight.

Amid the creeping-pine, which spreads
  Its thick and verdant wreath,
The scauberry's downy spangle sheds
  Its rich, delicious breath.
The bee-swarm murmurs by, and now
It clusters black on yonder bough:
  The robin's mottled breast
Glances that sunny spot across,
As round it seeks the twig and moss
  To frame its summer nest.

Warmer shines each successive sky,
  More soft the breezes pass,
The maple's flowers of crimson lie
  Upon the thick, green grass.
The elm has showered its fringes down,
The alder drops its tassels brown,
  Cowslips are by the rill;
The thrasher whistles in the glen,
Flutters around the warbling wren,
  And swamps have voices shrill.

A simultaneous burst of leaves
  Next sheds an emerald glow:
A single day's bright sunshine weaves
  This vivid, gorgeous show.
Masses of shade are cast beneath,

The flowers are spread in varied wreath ;
  Night brings its soft, sweet moon ;
Morn wakes in mist, and twilight gray
Weeps its bright dew, and smiling May
  Melts blooming into June !

TO ——.

THOU of the soft bright eye and raven hair,
Parted in glossy curves upon a brow
White as the ocean-pearl ; I gaze on thee
Until I am unconscious of aught else.
I look into the depth of that dark eye,
Upon the tablet of that glorious brow,
And read the gentle thoughts of thy pure heart ;
Then turn away with loathing from myself,
That I should mingle in the sins of earth
When such a being treads it. As thy form
Moves in its perfect gracefulness, it seems
Made but to float to music, and I feel
My pulses bounding wildly. I have hung
Upon the silvery accents of thy voice,
And thought that sweeter melody ne'er met
The ear of man, although in olden times
He heard the tongue of Angels. Melting strains
O'er moonlit waters, are most like thy tones
When sadness broods upon thee, and thy laugh,
Ringing so light and merrily from the heart,
Is joyous as the bluebird's blithsome song
When Spring wakes up the flowers ; and thy sweet
face

Is radiant, as with sunshine brightening o'er.
I 've watched the motions of thy rich red lips
Dropping their music-words, until I longed
To be invisible, that I might touch
Their rosiness unchidden.

O how bright
Beams Woman in her beauty! she combines
All charms possessed of Nature ; the light cloud
Wreathing its folds across the smiling blue
Is not more graceful than her gliding tread ;
The gem is not more brilliant than her eye ;
The bird's note more melodious than her voice ;
She is a shrine where man should bow him down,
Forget his paltry mean-souled love of self,
And in the sunlight of her purity
See the dark shadows of his own vile heart.
Thus, gentle lady ! do I kneel to thee ;
And in thy sweet and gentle influence
Strive with the passions that consume my life,
Turn from the sins that weigh my spirit down,
And walk the path made holy by thy tread.

SONG FOR INDEPENDENCE.

HAIL to this planting of Liberty's tree !
Hail to the charter declaring us free !
Millions of voices are chanting its praises,
  Millions of worshippers bend at its shrine,
Wherever the sun of America blazes,
  Wherever the stars of our bright banner shine.

Sing to the heroes who breasted the flood
That swelling, rolled o'er them — a deluge of blood.
Fearless they clung to the ark of the nation,
  And dashed on mid lightning, and thunder, and blast,
Till Peace, like the dove, brought her branch of salvation,
  And Liberty's mount was their refuge at last.

Bright smiles the beautiful land of our birth,
The home of the homeless all over the earth.
Oh ! let us ever with fondest devotion,
  The freedom our fathers bequeathed us, watch o'er,
Till the Angel shall stand on the earth and the ocean,
  And shout o'er earth's ruins, that Time is no more.

THE LOST HUNTER.

NUMBED by the piercing, freezing air,
  And burdened by his game,
The Hunter, struggling with despair,
  Dragged on his shivering frame ;
The rifle he had shouldered late
Was trailed along, a weary weight,
  His pouch was void of food,
The hours were speeding in their flight,
And soon the long, keen, winter night
  Would wrap the solitude.

Oft did he stoop a listening ear,
  Sweep round an anxious eye,
No bark or axe-blow could he hear,
  No human trace descry.
His sinuous path, by blazes, wound
Among the trees in myriad round;
  By naked boughs, between
Whose tangled architecture, fraught
With many a shape grotesquely wrought,
  The hemlock's spire was seen.

An antlered dweller of the wild
  Had met his eager gaze,

And far his wandering steps beguiled
  Within an unknown maze;
Stream, rock, and runway he had crossed,
Unheeding, till the signs were lost
  That guided once his roam;
And now, deep swamp and wild ravine,
And rugged mountain were between
  The Hunter and his home.

A dusky haze, which slow had crept
  On high, now darkened there,
And a few snow-flakes fluttering swept
  Athwart the thick gray air:
Faster and faster, till between
The trunks and boughs a mottled screen
  Of glimmering motes was spread;
That ticked against each object round
With gentle and continuous sound,
  Like brook o'er pebbled bed.

The laurel tufts, that drooping hung
  Close rolled around their stems,
And the sear beech-leaves still that clung,
  Were white with powdering gems.
But hark! afar a sullen moan
Swelled out to louder, deeper tone,
  As, surging near, it passed;
And bursting with a roar and shock,
That made the groaning forest rock,
  On rushed the winter blast.

As o'er it whistled, shrieked, and hissed,
  Caught by its swooping wings,
The snow was whirled to eddying mist,
  That seem'd as barbed with stings;
And now 't was swept with lightning flight
Above the loftiest hemlock's height,
  Like driving smoke, and now
It hid the air with shooting clouds,
And robed the trees with circling shrouds,
  Then dashed in heaps below.

Here, plunging in a billowy wreath,
  There, clinging to a limb,
The suffering hunter gasped for breath,
  Brain reeled and eye grew dim ;
As though to whelm him in despair,
Rapidly changed the blackening air
  To murkiest gloom of night,
Till naught was seen around, below,
But falling flakes, and mantled snow
  That gleamed in ghastly white.

At every blast an icy dart
  Seemed through his nerves to fly,
The blood was freezing to his heart,
  Thought whispered he must die.
The thundering tempest echoed death,
He felt it in his tightened breath,
  Spoil, rifle dropped, and slow
As the dread torpor crawling came

Along his staggering, stiffening frame,
  He sank upon the snow.

Reason forsook her shattered throne;
  He deemed that summer hours
Again around him brightly shone
  In sunshine, leaves, and flowers:
Again the fresh, green forest sod,
Rifle in hand, he lightly trod,—
  He heard the deer's low bleat;
Or, couched within the shadowy nook,
He drank the crystal of the brook
  That murmured at his feet.

It changed: his cabin-roof o'erspread,
  Rafter, and wall, and chair
Gleamed in the crackling fire, that shed
  Its warmth, and he was there;
His wife had clasped his hand, and now
Her gentle kiss was on his brow;
  His child was prattling by;
The hound crouched, dozing, near the blaze,
And through the pane's frost-pictured haze
  He saw the white drifts fly.

That passed: before his swimming sight
  Does not a figure bound,
And a soft voice with wild delight
  Proclaim the lost is found?
No, Hunter, no! 't is but the streak

Of snow, — 't is but the tempest's shriek, —
  No human aid is near ;
Never again that form will meet
Thy clasped embrace, those accents sweet
  Speak music to thine ear.

Morn broke : away the clouds were chased ;
  The sky shone pure and bright ;
And on its blue, the branches traced
  Their webs of glittering white.
Its ivory roof the hemlock stooped,
The pine its silvery tassels drooped,
  Down bent the burdened wood ;
And scattered round, low points of green
Peering above the snowy scene,
  Told where the thickets stood.

In a deep hollow, drifted high,
  A wave-like heap was thrown ;
Dazzlingly in the sunny sky
  A diamond blaze it shone ;
The little snow-bird chirping sweet
Dotted it o'er with tripping feet ;
  Unsullied, smooth, and fair
It seemed like other mounds, where trunk
And rock amid the wreaths were sunk,
  But oh ! the dead was there !

Spring came with skies and breezes bland,
  Soft suns and melting rains ;

And roused by her transforming wand,
  Earth burst its winter chains.
In a deep nook, where moss, and grass,
And fern-leaves wove a verdant mass —
  Some scattered bones beside,
A mother kneeling with her child
Told by her tears and wailings wild
  That there the lost had died.

A FOREST WALK.

A LOVELY sky, a cloudless sun,
  A wind that breathes of leaves and flowers,
O'er hill, through dale, my steps have won,
  To the cool forest's shadowy bowers ;
One of the paths, all round that wind
  Traced by the browsing herds, I choose,
And sights and sounds of human kind,
  In Nature's lone recesses lose ;
The beech displays its marbled bark,
  The spruce its green tent stretches wide,
While scowls the hemlock, grim and dark,
  The maple's scalloped dome beside :
All weave on high a verdant roof,
That keeps the very sun aloof,
Making a twilight soft and green
Within the columned, vaulted scene.

Sweet forest odors have their birth
From the clothed boughs and teeming earth ;
Where pine-cones dropped, leaves piled and dead,
  Long tufts of grass and stars of fern,
  With many a wild-flower's fairy urn
A thick, elastic carpet spread ;
Here, with its mossy pall, the trunk,
Resolving into soil, is sunk ;

There, wrenched but lately from its throne,
  By some fierce whirlwind circling past,
Its huge roots massed with earth and stone,
  One of the woodland kings is cast.

Above, the forest tops are bright
With the broad blaze of sunny light:
But now, a fitful air-gust parts
  The screening branches, and a glow
Of dazzling, startling radiance darts
  Down the dark stems, and breaks below;
The mingled shadows off are rolled,
The sylvan floor is bathed in gold:
Low sprouts and herbs, before unseen,
Display their shades of brown and green;
Tints brighten o'er the velvet moss,
Gleams twinkle on the laurel's gloss;
The robin, brooding in her nest,
Chirps as the quick ray strikes her breast,
And as my shadow prints the ground,
I see the rabbit upward bound,
With pointed ears an instant look,
Then scamper to the darkest nook,
Where, with crouched limb and staring eye,
He watches while I saunter by.

A narrow vista carpeted
With rich green grass, invites my tread;
Here showers the light in golden dots,
There sleeps the shade in ebon spots,
So blended, that the very air

Seems network as I enter there.
The partridge, whose deep-rolling drum
  Afar has sounded on my ear.
Ceasing its beatings as I come,
  Whirrs to the sheltering branches near;
The little milk-snake glides away,
The brindled marmot dives from day;
And now, between the boughs, a space
Of the blue laughing sky I trace;
On each side shrinks the bowery shade;
Before me spreads an emerald glade;
The sunshine steeps its grass and moss,
That couch my footsteps as I cross;
Merrily hums the tawny bee,
The glittering humming-bird I see;
Floats the bright butterfly along,
The insect choir is loud in song;
A spot of light and life, it seems
A fairy haunt for fancy dreams.

  Here stretched, the pleasant turf I press,
In luxury of idleness;
Sun-streaks, and glancing wings, and sky
Spotted with cloud-shapes, charm my eye;
While murmuring grass, and waving trees,
Their leaf-harps sounding to the breeze;
And water-tones that tinkle near,
Blend their sweet music to my ear;
And by the changing shades alone,
The passage of the hours is known.

JANUARY AND JUNE.

A SABLE pall of sky: the billowy hills
Swathed in the snowy robe that Winter throws
So kindly over Nature; skeleton trees
Fringed with rich, silver drapery, and the stream
Dumb in its frosty chains. Yon rustic bridge
Bristles with icicles; beneath it stand
The cattle-group, long pausing while they drink
From the ice-hollowed pools that skim in sheets
Of delicate glass, and shivering as the air
Cuts with keen, stinging edge; and those gaunt trunks
Bending with ragged branches o'er the bank,
Seem, with their mocking scarfs of chilling white,
Mourning for the green grass and fragrant flowers,
That Summer mirrors in the rippling flow
Of the bright stream below them. Shrub and rock
Are carved in pearl, and the dense thicket shows
Clusters of purest ivory. Comfortless
The frozen scene, yet not all desolate.
Where slopes, by tree and bush, the beaten track,
The sleigh glides merrily, with prancing steeds,
And the low homestead, nestling by its grove,
Clings to the leaning hill.

The drenching rain
Had streamed, and then, the large loose flakes had
showered,
Quick freezing where they fell; and thus the scene,
By Winter's alchemy, from gleaming steel
Was changed to sparkling silver.
Yet, though bright
And rich, the landscape smiles with lovelier look
When Summer gladdens it. The fresh blue sky
Bends, like God's blessing, o'er; the scented air
Echoes with bird-songs, and the emerald grass
Blinks, dappled with quick shadows; the light wing
Of the soft west makes music in the leaves;
The ripples murmur as they dance along;
The thicket, by the road-side, casts its cool
Black breadth of shade across the heated dust;
The cattle seek the pools beneath the banks,
Where sport the gnat-swarms glancing in the sun, —
Gray, whirling specks, — and darts the dragon-fly,
A gold-green arrow; and the wandering sheep
Nibble the short, thick sward, that clothes the brink,
Down sloping to the waters. Kindly tones
And happy faces make the homestead walls
A paradise. Upon the mossy roof
The tame dove coos and bows; beneath the eaves
The swallow frames her nest; the social wren
Lights on the flower-lined paling, and trills through
Its noisy gamut; and the humming-bird
Shoots, with that flying harp, the honey-bee,
Mid the trailed honeysuckle's trumpet-bloom.

Sunset wreathes gorgeous shapes within the west,
To eyes that love the splendor ; morning wakes
Light hearts to joyous tasks ; and when deep night
Breathes o'er the earth a solemn solitude,
With stars for watchers, or the holy moon
A sentinel upon the steeps of heaven,
Smooth pillows yield their balm to prayer and trust ;
And slumber, that sweet medicine of toil,
Sheds her soft dews and weaves her golden dreams.

THE LATE HON. STEPHEN VAN RENSSELAER.

TOWERING on high, a mighty oak
  Stood, monarch of the scene,
On which revolving summers woke
  A thicker, fresher green.
Beneath its arms, stretched grandly round,
The humblest plants protection found
  From every chilling air ;
And even the eagle, sweeping by,
Stooped to its top with kindling eye,
  And built its eyrie there.

It bent not to the winter blast,
  The lightning spared its dart ;
Time seamed its rugged bark, but cast
  No wither on its heart ;
Although the eagle claimed its crest,
Its green sprays held the robin's nest,
  And tiny forms and wings
Gleamed round : 't was beautiful to see
That oak, with all its majesty,
  So loved by lovely things.

But now no more came leafy bloom,
  The lichen stained its trunk,
And, bending to the general doom,
  In death it calmly sunk.
No wrenching storm the trophy won,
But fanned by breeze, and decked by sun,
  It sought its native earth,
Which, like a mother, threw across
The soft green robe of grass and moss
  With which she wrapped its birth.

The human oak, — the great, the strong
  Thus towered amid his race ;
And every year that swept along
  But brought a lovelier grace ;
He caused "the widow's heart to sing,"
And took from Poverty its sting,
  From Sorrow its despair ;
And when the war-cry echoed dread,
Fame's Eagle, stooping to his head,
  Entwined the laurel there.

Adversity's relentless storm
  (And all feel human ill)
Ne'er left a trace upon his form,
  Nor on his heart a chill ;
Though crowned by Fame, yet in his breast
Each pure affection was a guest,
  High thought and noble trust :
All saw and blessed that towering one

Basking in fortune's brightest sun,—
  So gentle, kind, and just.

But now, Time clothed that head with white,
  And bent that stately frame,
And, like eve merging into night,
  Death, robed in friendship, came.
Oh not with fear and anguish deep,
But calmly fell he into sleep,
  As Summer's sun departs ;
Men held their breath with awe, when first
Upon their ears the tidings burst,
  Then stamped him on their hearts.

AN OCTOBER RAMBLE.

A GLORIOUS afternoon : the moving shades
Have wheeled their slow half-circles, pointing now
Toward the sunshiny east ; a shadowy haze
Trembles amid the azure overhead,
Deepening to purple at the horizon's skirts.
Nature is smiling sweetly, and my feet
Are wandering in the pleasant woods once more.
Keen nights have told of Winter on his way,
And Autumn from the dark gaunt trees has drawn
(Save a few shreds upon the beech and oak)
His gorgeous robe, and cast it o'er the earth
For Indian Summer's glimmering form to rest
Awhile upon it, ere the blighting frost
And muffling snow. More golden is the sun
Than in its summer radiance, and it throws
Its charm on all around. Along this path
I tread, light-hearted, glad to be alone
With Nature. Beautiful and grand art thou !
Man with his passions dims thy light, his voice
Jars with thy sounds, his walls and towers but mar
Thy proud, exhaustless glory. Solitude,
With its soft, dreamy silence, is the mate
The fittest for thee, visible smile of God.

I gaze around me: trunks and boughs and leaves!
The robin on yon dog-wood's branch I see
Picking the crimson berries; now and then
The flicker drops his hammer on the bark,
And the soft echo starts, as breaks on high
The hoarse voice of the sluggish passing crow.
My foot stirs up the oval butternut
From the dead leaves, its dark brown tinged with
 gold,
And strewed around this old oak's knotted roots
Are acorn chalices, with braided sides,
Left by the fays to fill their depths with dew
For the next moonlight revel on the moss.
That strange awakener at Winter's verge,
The low witch-hazel, shows its yellow stars
Curled thick along its boughs; yon tall, slim plant
Dangles with blossoms, like a Chinese tower
Pendent with bells; and this blue gentian, tight
Has twisted the fringed rim of its long cup,
To keep from frost the topaz set within.
The air is richest perfume from the fern,
Sweetest when dying, like a virtuous life
Diffusing its example at its close.
I pluck a branch: what delicate tracery
Of veins minute! and see upon its back
The seeds, in brown and regular array
Secreted, as the partridge hides her young
Under her wings. Yon aster, that displayed
A brief while since its gorgeous bloom, has now
Around the shells that multiply its life

Woven soft downy plumes. How wonderful
And perfect is thy care, O Thou most high
Creator, Father, God! The flower and man
Protected equally by Thee.
The woods
Are left, and hills and glades and fields are round.
Yon piny knoll, thick covered with the brown
Dead fringes, in the sunshine's bathing flood
Looks like dark gold. From every tip of grass
And plant, a web of gossamer is stretched
Far as the eye can see, with varying hues
Shooting and shifting quick along the threads.
The sun now rests upon the western ridge
That seems dissolving in a golden haze
Where rests his blazing circle: as he sinks,
The haze melts off; rich purple clothes the mount,
The brief gray twilight brings the scattered stars,
And soon upwheels the full broad Hunter's moon,
Shedding her affluent silver o'er the earth.

A CONTRAST.

A LAKE lies slumbering in the wild-wood depths,
Picturing naught upon its polished glass
But the long-stretching and contracting shades
That change as change the hours : its sullen tones
Blending but with the forest's daylight songs
And midnight howlings ; o'er the leafy waste
Curls a light thread of smoke, — a hunter's fire ;
And mid the lilies' floating golden globes,
Spangling the margin, where the ripples play
And melt in silver, rocks his bark canoe.

A few years circle by. The talisman
Of toil has waved above this forest-scene.
Rich meadows, spotted with dense waving woods,
Slope to the sunlit surface of the lake,
Whose dashings mingle with the village-din,
And rural low and bleat. Where curled that smoke
Glitter white walls, and cluster roofs of men,
With terraced gardens, leaning to the wave,
Religion rearing spires, and Learning, domes
To the bright skies that arch this Eden-spot.
The rude canoe has vanished, but swift keels
Move joyous o'er the smiling, sparkling flood
That lies in calm obedience at the feet
Of those that freed it from its dungeon-shades.

THE FALLS OF THE MONGAUP.[1]

STRUGGLING along the mountain path,
We hear, amid the gloom,
Like a roused giant's voice of wrath,
A deep-toned, sullen boom:
Emerging on the platform high,
Burst sudden to the startled eye
Rocks, woods, and waters, wild and rude, —
A scene of savage solitude.

Swift as an arrow from the bow,
Headlong the torrent leaps,
Then tumbling round, in dazzling snow
And dizzy whirls it sweeps;
Then, shooting through the narrow aisle
Of this sublime cathedral pile,
Amid its vastness, dark and grim,
It peals its everlasting hymn.

Pyramid on pyramid of rock
Tower upward wild and riven,

[1] The Falls of the Mongaup are in Sullivan county, New York, in the heart of the forest.

As piled by Titan hands to mock
    The distant smiling heaven.
And where its blue streak is displayed,
Branches their emerald network braid
So high, the eagle in his flight
Seems but a dot upon the sight.

Here columned hemlocks point in air
    Their cone-like fringes green;
Their trunks hang knotted, black, and bare,
    Like spectres o'er the scene;
Here, lofty crag and deep abyss,
And awe-inspiring precipice;
There, grottos bright in wave-worn gloss,
And carpeted with velvet moss.

No wandering ray e'er kissed with light
    This rock-walled sable pool,
Spangled with foam-gems thick and white,
    And slumbering deep and cool;
But where yon cataract roars down,
Set by the sun, a rainbow crown
Is dancing o'er the dashing strife,—
Hope glittering o'er the storm of life.

Beyond, the smooth and mirrored sheet
    So gently steals along,
The very ripples, murmuring sweet,
    Scarce drown the wild bee's song;

The violet from the grassy side
Dips its blue chalice in the tide ;
And, gliding o'er the leafy brink,
The deer, unfrightened, stoops to drink.

Myriads of man's time-measured race
    Have vanished from the earth,
Nor left a memory of their trace,
    Since first this scene had birth ;
These waters, thundering now along,
Joined in Creation's matin-song ;
And only by their dial-trees
Have known the lapse of centuries !

A DREAM.

A SIMPLE sprig of myrtle! As the stem,
Clustered with dark-green glossy leaves, was placed
Within my grasp, gay visions and bright scenes
Thronged round me as by magic; the soft spell
Of music had been cast upon my soul,
Melting it with delicious cadences
Dying upon the ear, or with swift flights
Bearing it upward, as on wings, to heaven.
Beautiful forms were floating in the dance;
Beings, whose looks of radiant loveliness
Were blended, like the rainbow, in one blaze
Of ravishing splendor: here, the laughing eye
Tinged with the hue that robes the violet;
And there, the large bright orb of ebony
Kindling quick flame where'er its glances fell.
Yet, as I gazed upon the glossy gift,
The present vanished from me, and above
The glowing, glorious sky of Italy, —
So glowing, and so glorious, Fancy well
Might deem it the spread garment of the sun, —
Shone in its beauty; olive vales spread out,
And myrtle bowers sprung round me; ivied walls
And mouldering columns stood before my eye:

While, in the distance, like a sapphire, gleamed
Bright Maggioré dotted with its isles.
I lived, I breathed in that rich purple clime,
Where Life's bright cup is brimmed with sparkling
joys,
That steep the soul in deepest happiness.
And then I thought those beautiful dark eyes
Beaming beside me, full of light and soul,
Were glittering underneath that brilliant heaven,
Which the magnificent southern moon had made
One sheet of silver ; and that clustering hair,
Black as the raven's plumage, was entwined
With Italy's green myrtle wreaths and flowers ;
And the sweet tones of that infectious laugh
Were sounding o'er the spangled waters, blent
With the low music of the light guitar,
As the swift gondola darted on its way.

And then the vision changed. I was in Spain.
Slopes, mantled with their vineyards, rose around;
The lemon gleamed, a spot of gold, among
Its polished foliage; streams, like silvery threads,
Glittered mid bordering spires ; while high, afar,
The Pyrenees, like giant-monarchs stood,
With crowns of silver, and with purple robes,
As if to guard this scene of loveliness.
The air seemed peopled with the gay Antique
That witnessed the Alhambra in its pride,
Grenada's golden towers, and all the bright
And gorgeous scenes of vanished chivalry.

Within a pleasant glade, upon whose grass
The cork-tree threw its shadow, I beheld
A group of peasants dancing.

Then I thought
Thy buoyant, graceful step was bounding free
Within the mazes of that merry dance
To the light clicking of the castanet:
And as the hours flew by, and radiant Day
Sank prostrate on the snow of some high peak,
With crimson mantle, and with golden plume,
While boughs gave birth to shadows, and the air,
Rich with the orange fragrance, bore along
The silvery ringing of the Spanish bell
From some far convent, and the vesper hymn
Floated o'er Guadalquiver's glittering breast;
I deemed that thou wert straying by the side
Of that weird stream, whose sands are made of gold,
Like that of olden fable, listening deep
To the wild tales of those high passionate hearts,
That beat so fiercely in the battle-storm,
And throbbed so fondly to the thoughts of love.
And as the Eve rose darkling from the West,
And looked upon thee with her diamond eye,
Palpable images of those days came:
The turbaned Moor upon his war-steed bore
His lance in rest, and on his breast his lyre;
Pennon, and scarf, and falchion flashed; the knight
Knelt at the feet of his fair "ladye-love,"
Castles frowned blackly o'er the mountain-pass,

And palaces gleamed brightly in the sun.
The vision thus was glowing, wrapping up
My thoughts and feelings, when a jesting word
Uttered by some gay passer-by, destroyed
The fairy happy spell, and I awoke.
The waltz was circling by me, and again
Music, with her invisible feet, now crept
Slowly and softly, and now bounded high
With her gay promptings, and I dream'd no more.

BRADY'S LEAP.

The following incident occurred in the year 1780. The individual referred to was Captain Samuel Brady, a noted hunter and Indian fighter, in the region about the Ohio River.

A STRIPE of sky its sunshine threw
  Upon a sylvan glade,
On which the circling forest drew
  Its pictured shapes of shade ;
'T was spotted with low thickets, where
Throbbed the faint pulses of the air,
  Beatings of Nature's sleep ;
Beside, no motion of a thing,
Nor chirp, nor flutter of a wing,
  Came o'er the stillness deep.

But now, far shouts and steps were heard
  Within the forest's breast,
Approaching nearer, till the bird
  Flew frightened from its nest ;
Till bough, and moss, and grass were rife
With myriad throngs of tiny life
  Circling and murmuring round ;
And the whole scene, so lately still,
In leaping forms and voices shrill,
  Woke startled at the sound.

With laugh, and yell of joy, and hate,
  A savage group burst in,
Like demons met to celebrate
  A festival of sin.
Some stripped a neighboring sapling bare,
Some dragged and bound a white man there,
  And round him branches piled ;
While all keen knife and hatchet grasped,
With eyes that glowed, and breasts that gasped
  To hold their orgies wild.

Maddening for their fierce revelry,
  Still nearer pressed the throng,
Then burst in horrid mocking glee
  Loud whoop and boisterous song.
Woman's shrill tones and Manhood's shout
And childish shrieks rang echoing out,
  Upon the sunny air ;
But not a fear the lone one shook ;
He glanced around with lofty look,
  Undarkened by despair.

Through the piled boughs red streaks of flame
  Like darting serpents ran,
Still not a tremor thrilled the frame
  Of that bound, helpless man.
He viewed, with calm and equal breath,
The flashing curls of coming death ;
  The same in soul as though
His deadly rifle still he bore,

A dauntless hunter warrior,
  With bosom to the foe.

Now to the chant, in circling dance
  Writhed every bounding limb,
And every fiend-like countenance
  Grew still more black and grim;
Some whirled their hatchets round his head
With starting eyeballs burning red,
  And teeth with rage that gnashed;
Some scorched his shrinking skin with brands,
Or, blood-drops spirting o'er their hands,
  With knives his bosom gashed.

At length a mother, at whose breast
  A trembling infant clung,
Close to the suffering victim pressed
  With loud and scornful tongue.
A hope flashed o'er him: quick as thought,
With giant grasp the child he caught
  And hurled it in the blaze;
Then, as all rushed to where it lay,
He snapped the shrivelling thongs away,
  And vanished from their gaze.

Now, hunter, urge thy fleet career!
  Let not a muscle fail,
Like wolves that scent the flying deer,
  Swift feet are on thy trail;
Dash through the thicket, — leap the mound, —

Thy foemen's shoutings nearer sound, —
  On, on, pause not for breath !
A shot has grazed that sheltering tree ;
Rush down this steep declivity !
  For close behind is death.

Within the clustering swamp he springs
  To seek some darkened nook,
Now by the pendent hemlock swings
  Across the laurel-brook.
The bear from covert, snorting, wakes,
The snake his warning rattle shakes,
  But on the hunter flies ;
Breathless he climbs the broken hill,
Below, the foemen follow still,
  And still their war-whoops rise.

But now upon the burdened air
  Creeps a low, steady roar ;
The Cuyahoga tumbles there, —
  Hope lights his breast once more.
He knows the spot : through narrow rocks
The torrent beats with billowy shocks, —
  A war-horse clothed with white,
Thundering along its curbless way,
Flinging its mane-like showers of spray
  Athwart the yawning night.

One glance : above the hill's steep edge
  Ascending war-plumes float ;

He bounds to where a dizzy ledge
  Juts o'er the torrent's throat;
Nerving his strength one instant there,
His leaping figure cuts the air,
  The dread ravine is passed;
And, as the baffled foemen shrink
From the black chasm's terrific brink,
  His heart beats free at last.

Thick, screening branches, as they fly,
  Turn off the whizzing balls;
And now along the western sky
  The gold-fringed sunset falls.
And soon he saw Night's mantle black
Folded around his forest track,
  With friendly stars to guide;
And when Morn wove her dappled woof,
He sat beneath his cabin roof
  With glad ones at his side.

THE MILL.

Beside the narrow road that, winding, leads
From the broad arched highway, the humble mill
Rears its red-gabled front. The forest round
Has fallen beneath the axe, to shape the nook
For the sharp-pointed roof, and wood-built dam
Bridling the swampy streamlet to a pond,
Scattered with dead, jagged trees and splintered stumps,
And floating logs, round which the frothy scum
And drooping weeds are gathered. Stagnant, still,
And gloomy seems the wide-spread sheet, what time
The sliding gate is lowered: the slimy flume
Looks dark; the waters trickle o'er the dam,
Or gush from some wide fissure; and the mill
Is left to deepest silence. But when morn,
Bringing the daily task, uplifts the gate,
The scene, like magic, changes: the smooth pond
Breaks into slanting lines; the scum whirls round;
The rough, black logs sail, jostling, and the weeds
Stream in the dancing ripples; through the flume
The waters rush in foam, the dusky wheel
Whirls its huge circle, as the dashing flood
Leaps on its buckets; grate and hum succeed
Throughout the structure till the daylight dies.

We enter in: a thin white dust is spread
O'er walls, and bin, and floor; huge swelling sacks
Here, prone, or leaning each on each; there, raised
By sinewy hands on brawny backs, and brought
With staggering efforts to the porch, where stand
The broad-wheeled wagon, and the dozing steeds,
That now and then arouse to pick amid
The hay-mounds at their feet. The miller, bluff
And bustling, powdered thickly o'er with white,
Pours from the measure the bright golden corn,
Or dark brown buckwheat, in the hopper broad, —
A level mass that in its midst soon shows
A hollowed spot, as swift the particles
Drop to the crushing, grinding stones beneath, —
Till, funnel-shaped, the sliding load appears,
And the light grains at last whirl round the mouth
Of the deep passage, and quick disappear.
From the long tube, within the box beneath,
Streams the warm flour in readiness for the sack,
And a strong odor breathes like smitten flint,
Through the dim, dusty air.
                                        Familiar, rude,
And known to all, this picture of the mill.
Let all, then, heed the lesson. Industry
Hews its own place amid this crowded world;
And, standing in its humble path, sheds round
Life, comfort, by its presence. With a hand
That tires not, and a soul that never faints,
It brings prosperity around its home,
And glads the bosom with perpetual smiles.

THE FOREST TEMPLE.

GRAND pomp of the Wilderness! solemn and wild,
Magnificent temple, for Solitude piled!
Its columns the rocks, and its canopy, sky;
Its huge mountain-altar reared proudly on high.
Round circle the Seasons: Spring dances along,—
It is breathing with fragrance and vocal with song;
Its grass-carpet lifts to the steps of her showers;
At the wand of her sunbeam come thronging its flowers.
Bright, beautiful Summer her thick garland weaves,
And its depths are made dim with her mantle of leaves;
There is dancing of shadows in ebony gloss,
And gold-slants and sprinkles on blossom and moss.
Gay alchemist Autumn transmutes, and behold!
The emerald changed to rich crimson and gold;
There is glitter of gems,—a proud blazon of hues,
And silver mist forming, to melt with the dews;
The moon's splendor streams with more pomp from on high,
And the star-clusters glow with more light in the sky.
Wild Winter on rushes, ice-crystals its mail,

His war-steed the tempest; his arrows the hail;
The temple stands blighted and mute at his glance,
The glitter has faded, and past is the dance,
Till Spring, with her soft looks and sweet smiles, again
Breathes joy, as the Despot abandons his reign.

And music, sweet music, the temple gives forth
When Winter has reached his stern home in the North:
The torrent-like stream, as, mad-foaming, it bounds,
Loud raises, unceasing, its organ-like sounds;
There are voices of birds, and a murmur of bees,
And soft strains of wind-harps breathed low through the trees,
And thunder o'er-rolling, and launching its crash,
And the strong sheeted rains, as fierce downward they dash,
And the wild blast, as onward it rages and shoots,
Whirling boughs from their trees, — wrenching trees from their roots, —
The bird-song, — the blast hymn, — the chant of the flood,
Sent upward in praise to their Maker and God.

And other sounds forth, too, this temple hath cast,
Sounds loud as the thunder, and fierce as the blast;
When Tyranny's hordes, grasping fetters, were led
O'er a region that shuddered with wrath at their tread;

In an air that grew black, as their banners it fanned,
Till the fierce storm of Vengeance thick curtained the land.
'T was the war-shout of Freedom! and echoed by men
She poured down from mountain and rallied in glen,
As proudly she spread her pure flag for the fray,
And her young Eagle stretched his strong wings on her way.
Oh, what though to earth that starred banner was cast!
Oh, what though those wings were crushed down by the blast!
Brave hearts bore that banner, — 't was lifted anew;
High hopes cheered those pinions, — more lofty they flew;
Till Victory, loud as the roar of the sea,
In heart-bursts were shouted by men that were Free!

FOURTH OF JULY ODE.

Oh, what is that sound swelling loudly on high
Wherever our land shows its boundless dominions,
And uncurbed with the Stars and the Stripes, in the sky
Borne aloft by our flag, spreads our Eagle his pinions!
'T is an Empire's glad strain!
The Free, hailing again
The day, when their sires trod on sceptre and chain:
And proudly their sons will remember this day,
Till the last wave of time bears its glories away.

Oppression strode on; the cloud gathered o'erhead,
And Freedom beheld him, with scorn, from her station,
Our Eagle's fierce eye blazed with wrath at his tread,
Till the day that our land reared its front as a Nation.
Then the red lightning sprung,
Then the thunder-burst rung,
'T was the eye-flash of Freedom, — the sound of her tongue:
Then proudly her sons will remember this day,
Till the last wave of time bears its glories away.

In its field stood the plough; the axe ceased in the
wood;
From his log cabin gladly the wild hunter sallied;
From city and glen, throngs were poured like a flood,
To the flag where the ranks of the valiant were
rallied.
Oh, let Bunker's red height
And let Trenton's wild fight
Tell how nobly our sires bled and died for the right:
Then proudly their sons will remember this day,
Till the last wave of time bears its glories away.

On no happier clime than this broad land of ours,
Does the sun his bright smiles of beneficence
render;
From dark storms and bleak snows, to rich skies and
sweet flowers,
Our flag, our proud flag, streams in starred and
striped splendor;
Then with shouts of acclaim,
And with bosoms of flame,
Let us honor those sires whence our liberties came:
And proudly their sons will remember this day,
Till the last wave of time bears its glories away,

THE BEECH–TREE.

Dropped by the wind-kissed parent-spray,
  The brown nut, whence the beech-tree's birth,
Down trodden by the rabbit, lay
  Forming within the forest earth.
Urged by its secret principle,
At length from out its perished shell
  The sprout sought light and air;
And by the nibbling fawn unseen
Its downy stem grew firm and green,
  And rose a sapling there.

Its roots stretched out — its branches spread, —
  Thickened its trunk, until on high
Covered with leaves, its lofty head
  Made fretwork of its spot of sky.
A wand the robin bent, now stood
The giant monarch of the wood,
  Where paused the eagle's flight;
Once trembling at the slightest breath,
It now scarce deigned to stir, beneath
  The tempest's fiercest might.

The deer, amid its cool green gloom,
  Sought refuge from the noontide heat,

And sounding in its leafy dome
  The thrasher's warbled notes were sweet.
The sunbeams scarce could find their way
Through its thick screen, their dots to lay
  Upon the roots below
That wreathed deep mossy nooks, where led
The quail her brood, when Winter spread
  His chilling robes of snow.

And Nature's jewels, — radiant things,
  Loved the green sylvan place; the bee,
Turning to harps its quivering wings,
  With arrowy straightness sought the tree.
Floated the yellow butterfly,
A wandering spot of sunshine, by;
  And, nestling in its moss,
The sky-tinged violet's fairy cup
Its draught of fragrance offered up
  To airs that stole across.

Its branches formed the panther's lair
  When waiting for his deadly leap,
And in its hollowed trunk, the bear
  Coiled his black form in torpid sleep.
Ages of Springs renewed its crown,
Ages of Autumns cast it down,
  Till heaps on heaps were strown;
Lichens crept up its furrowed side,
Its very race of eagles died,
  But still it held its throne.

But its time came : its figure drooped,
  Leaves smiled no more in vernal days,
And threads of pale green moss were looped
  Around its dry and shrivelled sprays.
It stood, a spectre gaunt and bare,
Reaching a crooked arm in air,
  To court the lightning's dart;
Until the tempest stooped, and cast
Its red sulphureous bolt at last,
  And scorched it to the heart.

Then as the gust came whirling round,
  It shook from root to pinnacle,
And headlong, to the echoing ground
  It hurtling, crashing, thundering fell.
Melting away, the fractured trunk
To a green moss-mound slowly sunk,
  Until the soil crept o'er,
And by its solemn mystery
Took to itself the stately tree,
  Which once it proudly bore.

A WALK TO TIVOLI.[1]

THE clouds are floating silver, and the sky
So pure, the sight seems piercing up to heaven.
Distance has hushed the city's ceaseless din;
And now the warble of the robin sounds
From the near orchard; and the patriarch trees,
Shading the quaint old mansion with their leaves
And eloquent with the memories of one[2]
Upon whom smiled the angels, fix the eye.
Southward the river gleams; a snowy sail
Now gliding o'er its mirror, — now a track
Tossing with foam, displaying on its course
The graceful steamer with its flag of smoke.
Slopes swelling up in giant terraces
Dotted with trees, or purpled with thick woods,
With scattered roofs, and seamed with winding roads,
Frame this rich, beautiful picture to the East.
We leave the wheel-thronged thoroughfare; to the left
Fresh springs the summer grass, and light and soft,
It sinks beneath the footfall. Merrily
Dances the streamlet mid its sloping banks,
Now bright with dazzling jewelry, and now

1 A beautiful cascade in the Patroon's Creek, near Albany, N. Y.

2 The late Stephen Van Rensselaer.

Darkening with leafy coverts; mark yon bird,
Dipping its head and scattering silvery drops
By the quick flutterings of its tiny wings.

The quiet glade is passed, — the forest spreads
Its leafy wall, and in it winds the path.
Thick branches like a roof are stretched o'erhead,
Through which the sunshine falls in broken streaks,
And rains in golden sprinkles; here, the shade
Is sketched in fanciful lacework, hiding scarce
The chirping cricket; while its dense black mass
Would shelter, there, the partridge. Mossy roots
Are coiled around like serpents, and the fern
Shows its rich fluted wreath mid withered leaves
And sear red hemlock fringes, giving Earth
Her principle of life; with quick shrill chirp
Darts the striped squirrel in his fortress-bush,
Leaving his acorn to my crushing foot.
The odor of the dead wood scents the air,
And the soft winnowing wind comes stealthily
Breathing of sassafras.
The branching path
Here to the upland winds; there, plunges down
The sheer rough bank, to skirt the curving marge
Of the bright stream, whose waters pure and deep
Now broaden to a creek, so wide, yon duck
Skimming its surface dwindles in the midst
To a faint speck, and now is lost to sight
Upon its glossy sheet; below, a breath
Might urge the insect on its leaf across,

So narrow winds the passage ; here, the oar
Could freely dip, the canvas waft the bark
Before the breeze loud rushing through the pines.

We leave the shadowy woods ; a lovely glade
Opens upon us, and a deep-toned sound
Shakes on the ear ; it is the organ-voice
Of the hurled waters scattered o'er their rocks
In streaks of plunging foam, while high above
The twisted fir-tree slants as though to pitch
Headlong below.
The glade lies smooth and green,
Spangled with flowers, and gay with glancing shapes
And musical with songs, while on the eye
The ripples cast quick darts of blinding light.

Oh for the raven-haired and dark-eyed one !
To make this radiant scene more beautiful
With her sweet presence ; the bright sunshine then
Would glow more brightly, and this forest-rose
Breathe out a richer fragrance ; the green grass
Would rise up greener from her fairy tread,
And I would be in heaven ; a star would then
Gild my heart's depths with pure and holy ray,
And in the soul bright beaming from her eye
My spirit would find hope, and joy, and peace.

THE ISLAND.

UPON a narrow river-flat
The sunset falls in streaking glow;
Here, the mown meadow's velvet plat,
And there, the buckwheat's scented snow.
A cluster of low roofs is prest
Against the mountain's leaning breast.
But each rude porch is closed and barred:
For tenderest Youth and Age alone
Are left those humble roofs to guard,
Till Day resumes his blazing throne.

Where deepest shade the forest flings,
The hunters seek that forest's game;
Men tireless as the eagle's wings,
Of dauntless heart and iron frame.
The sparkling Beaverkill beside,[1]
Benighted in their wanderings wide,
They merry dress the slaughtered deer,
And make the twilight ring with cheer;
Now chorus of the woods, — now tale
Of panther-fight and Indian trail,

1 A romantic stream in Sullivan county, emptying into the Delaware.

Till the rude group, the camp-fire round,
Crouch with their rifles, on the ground.

Where wide the branch-linked river spreads,
  Near rapids swift, a fairy isle,
Three leagues above those mountain-sheds,
  Looks like a sweet perpetual smile.
The muskrat burrows in its sides,
Down its steep slopes the otter slides;
The splendid sheldrake, floating, feeds
In his close haunts amid the reeds;
Around its sandy points, all day,
Watches and wades the crane for prey;
While show its shallows lily-robes
Of heart-shaped leaves and golden globes.

Above the mountain hamlet, fade
Eve's tints, and darkness spreads its shade;
Their pointed tops the cedars rear
Against the starlight bright and clear.
Then come the many sounds and sights
Usual in forest summer-nights:
At intervals, the flitting breeze
Draws soft, low sobbings from the trees;
From the deep woods, in transient float,
Tinkles the whetsaw's double note;
The wakeful frog, unceasing, groans;
Twang the mosquito's hungry tones,
And echoing sweetly, on the hill,
Whistles the sorrowing whippoorwill;

From the cleft pine the gray owl hoots,
  Swells from the swamp the wolf's long cry,
And, now and then, a meteor shoots
  And melts within the spangled sky.
The fire-fly opes and shuts its gleam,
  The cricket chirps, the tree-toad crows ;
And hark ! the cougar's distant scream
  Afar the mountain echo throws.

What forms are those that crouch and creep
Around those roofs of happy sleep ?
The dim light falling from the sky
  Displays the tomahawk and knife :
Awake, awake within that lie
  In guardless rest, and arm for strife !
In vain : before each lowly porch
The savage grasps his glaring torch.
One moment, — then the warwhoops swell
Wild, fierce, terrific, yell on yell.
With blood cold curdling to the heart,
The inmates from their slumbers start ;
They wake, to hear the climbing flames
Roaring around their dwelling-frames, —
To see within the ruddy glare
The fierce foe mocking their despair.
The mother clasps her shrivelling child,
And shrieks her anguish shrill and wild ;
In strangling wreaths the old sire dies ;
They hush the maiden's frantic cries,

And matron gray and youthful bride
Burn in slow torture side by side.

What mean those clouds of rising smoke
  That streak the morning's dappled sky?
Alas, the ghastly sight that broke
  Upon each hunter's home-turned eye!
A heap of smouldering ashes now
Is seen beneath the mountain's brow;
While cindered bones and limbs round spread
In blackened fragments, tell the dead.

Another sunset, crouching low
  Upon a rising pile of cloud,
Bathes deep the island with its glow,
  Then shrinks behind its gloomy shroud.
From the sweet isle, loud chant and shout
Upon the heavy air ring out;
Rolling the twilight hours along
In orgies fierce, of dance and song,
The Indian warriors celebrate
Their last night's deed of vengeful hate,
Until the deep and frequent bowl
Has drowned in sleep each savage soul.

Trees plume the islet's utmost bound,
And tangled brushwood clothes the ground;
The leaves hang wilted on the sprays,
  By the fierce drought of August dried,

Until a spark might whelm in blaze
  That fairy islet's forest pride.
Deep midnight ; — loud the storm-wind's roar ;
  The hunters to the margin drew ;
And every brawny shoulder bore
  The burden of a light canoe.
What though on high before the blast,
The clouds, like sable waves, roll past,
They scorn the tempest's howling rage ;
Thoughts not of fear their minds engage,
But deep revenge on those that shed
Such bitter sorrow on their head.

The barks are launched ; they plunge and toss,
  Like bubbles on the swells are cast ;
But strong arms urge their flight across,
  The hunters reach the isle at last.
They listen : loud the ceaseless crash
With which the rapids onward dash ;
And deep the stern and steady roar
Of the thick pines on either shore ;
But on the isle, no human sound
Blends with the tempest's voices round.
Exhausted with their orgies, prone
To earth each savage form is thrown,
With not a guardian eye to keep
Its watch above that helpless sleep.

At narrow spaces round the isle
Each wary hunter rears his pile ;

Formed of the leaves and branches, cast
Beneath in myriads by the blast,
The loose sear masses stand on high, —
The smitten flints the sparks supply ;
The kindled flames like lightnings leap,
A furnace seems each glowing heap,
And guided by the light, once more
The barks are pointed to the shore.

Through the thick smoke break streaks of red ;
To lurid masses quick they spread ;
Each tree points up, a crimson spire ;
  Below, fierce rolling surges gleam,
Until a glaring isle of fire
  Crackles and roars upon the stream.
Keen ears are listening on the shore
With vengeful joy to that dread roar,
And watchful eyes beholding there
Those billows tossing in the air.
Once to their sight a figure came,
Wrapped in a sheet of clinging flame,
And with a shrill and horrid scream,
Plunged headlong in the dashing stream.

Morn glows: there hangs a brooding pall
Over that islet, shrouding all ;
The pigeon from his perch on shore
His monotone coos o'er and o'er;
The thrasher in the tamarack
  Calls echo up in varied sound,

And gliding on his run-way track
  The shy deer seeks his grazing-ground.
Tones on the sprays, scents on the winds!
Each thing of Nature pleasure finds
In the bright beams — the sweet bland air —
  Save that black smoking isle,
Changed to a waste of deep despair,
  From its sweet radiant smile.

THE PIONEER.

THROUGH the deep wilderness, where scarce the sun
Can cast his darts, along the winding path
The Pioneer is treading. In his grasp
Shines his keen axe, that wondrous instrument,
That, like the fabled talisman, transforms
Deserts to fields and cities. He has left
The home in which his early years were passed,
And led by hope, and full of restless strength,
Has plunged within the forest, there to plant
His destiny. Beside some rapid stream
He rears his log-walled cabin. When the chains
Of winter fetter Nature, and no sound
Disturbs the echoes of the dreary woods,
Save when some stem cracks sharply with the frost,
Then merrily rings his axe, and tree on tree
Crashes to earth; and when the long keen night
Mantles the wilderness in solemn gloom,
He sits beside his ruddy hearth, and hears
The wolf fierce snarling at the cabin door,
Or through the lowly casement sees his eye
Gleam like a burning coal.
                                        Spring's out-post, March,
Before the wood-snows melt, with warm bright days

And frosty nights, calls up the kindly sap
From the hard maple's roots; with care he wounds
The seamy bark, and drop by drop wells out
The sweet and limpid fluid, and his art
Fashions the rich dark sugar.
Now in piles
The prostrate trees are drawn, and upward flash
The fallow fires; and when the fiery storm
Has died in ashes, and the earth has cooled,
His voice sounds cheerly as the gliding plough
Turns the loose soil between the blackened stumps.
Then to the kindly earth and elements
Is left the harrowed seed. Time passes on,
And rich green tinges show the rising grain.
And when the autumn film is in the air,
Stalks, long and slender, rippling to the breeze,
And nodding, plump with wealth, reward the toil
Of the unwearied sower. The low barn
Receives the tawny loads, while in the fields
Points the hay-barrack. As the gradual smile
Thus steals, with brightening change, o'er Nature's face,
From the far settlement he brings in joy
A partner to his hearth. Years roll along.
Where stood the hut, a white walled cottage now
Looks through its screen of roses. Meadows stretch
With grain fields round. A village clusters near,
In whose broad street is heard a mingled din
Of saw and hammer, wagon-wheel and voice.
By the swift streamlet hums the busy mill,

And whirrs the bustling, long-roofed factory.
As the low sinking sun with magic brush
Paints the rich scene in stripes of black and gold,
Beneath the tree, where, through the first long night
He slept upon the spot his watch-fire blazed
To guard him from the panther, smiling sits
The white-haired Pioneer, while round him throng
Manhood and youth, and merry infancy,
Those whom his parent-hand had reared, and those
That call him grandsire. Far and wide he sees
The wonders he has caused: the bloom — the life —
Which glanced in broken visions through his brain
That night beneath the branches: and as dips
The sun within the west, he humbly hopes
His sun will sink as gently to the tomb,
And rise as brightly to eternal day.

The Spirit of our land, personified,
Is the bold Pioneer: that Spirit strong
And restless, which hath mowed its sinewy way
Along the forests, since the primal tree
Stooped to the axe-blow. Onward still it moves.
The Mississippi long hath heard its song,
The dark Missouri in her windings far
Hath borne its bark. Across the boundless plains
That roll their billows to "The Shining Heights,"
It wandering treads. The sentry prairie-dog
Alarms the burrowed city with his cry
At its approaching form. The wild Pawnee,
Borne like the wind upon his fiery steed,

Spearing the buffalo, with wonder sees
Its brow of ashy hue. The trapper rude,
Snaring the beaver by its lonely pond,
Melts into tears as accents he had known
In boyhood meet his ear.
The snowy peaks
Are passed, and still it struggles dauntless on,
Following the sun, till broad Pacific's breast
Shall gird its progress, and proclaim its bounds.

THE FRESHET.

A LEGEND OF THE DELAWARE.

MARCH hath unlocked stern Winter's chain ;
  Nature is wrapped in misty shrouds,
And ceaselessly the drenching rain
  Drips from the gray, sky-mantling clouds ;
The deep snows melt, and swelling rills
Pour through each hollow of the hills ;
The river from its rest hath risen,
And bounded from its shattered prison ;
The huge ice-fragments onward dash,
With grinding roar and splintering crash ;
Swift leap the floods upon their way,
  Like war-steeds thundering on their path,
With hoofs of waves and manes of spray,
  Restrainless in their mighty wrath.

Wild mountains stretch in towering pride
Along the river's either side ;
Leaving between it and their walls
Narrow and level intervals.
When Summer glows, how sweet and bright
The landscape smiles upon the sight ?

Here, the bright golden wheat-fields vie
With the rich tawny of the rye;
The buckwheat's snowy mantles, there,
Shed honeyed fragrance on the air;
In long straight ranks the corn uprears
Its silken plumes and pennoned spears;
The yellow melon, underneath
Plump ripens, in its viny wreath;
Here, the piled rows of new-mown grass;
There, the potato-plant's green mass;
All framed by woods, — each limit shown
By zigzag rail, or wall of stone;
Contrasting, here, within the shade,
The axe a space hath open laid,
Cumbered with trees hurled blended down,
Their verdure changed to withered brown;
There, the soil, ashes-strewed and black,
Shows the red flame's devouring track;
Slim fire-weeds shooting thick where stood
The leafy monarchs of the wood:
A landscape frequent in the land,
  Which Freedom, with her gifts to bless,
Grasping the axe when sheathing brand,
  Hewed from the boundless wilderness.

The rains have ceased: the struggling glare
Of sunset lights the misty air;
The fierce winds sweep the myriad throng
Of broken ragged clouds along;
From the rough saw-mill, where hath rung,

Through all the hours, its grating tongue,
The raftman sallies, as the gray
Of evening tells the flight of day,
And slowly seeks with loitering stride,
His cabin by the river side.
As twilight darkens into night,
Still dash the waters in their flight,
Still the ice-fragments, thick and fast,
Shoot like the clouds before the blast.

Beyond — the sinuous channel wends
Through a deep, narrow gorge, and bends
With curve so sharp, the drifting ice,
  Hurled by the flood's tremendous might,
Piles the opposing precipice,
  And every fragment swells the height;
Hour after hour uprears the wall,
Until a barrier huge and tall
Breasts the wild waves that vain upswell
To overwhelm the obstacle:
They bathe the alder on the verge,
The leaning hemlock now they merge,
The stately elm is dwindling low
Within the deep ingulfing flow,
Till curbed thus in its headlong flight,
With its accumulated might,
The river, turning on its track,
Rolls its broad-spreading volumes back.

The raftman slumbers; through his dream

Distorted visions wildly stream :
Now in the wood his axe he swings,
And now his saw-mill's jarring rings ;
Now his huge raft is shooting swift
Cochecton's wild, tumultuous rift,
Now floats it on the ebon lap
Of the grim shadowed Water Gap,
And now 't is tossing on the swells
Fierce dashing down the slope of Wells.
The rapids crash upon his ear,
The deep sounds roll more loud and near,
They fill his dream, — he starts, — he wakes !
  The moonlight through the casement falls,
Ha ! the wild sight that on him breaks, —
  The floods sweep round his cabin-walls.
Beneath their bounding, thundering shocks
The frail log fabric groans and rocks ;
Crash, crash ! the ice-bolts round it shiver ;
The walls like blast-swept branches quiver ;
His wife is clinging to his breast,
The child within his arm is prest,
He staggers through the chilly flood
That numbs his limbs, and checks his blood.
On, on he strives : the waters lave
Higher his form with every wave ;
They steep his breast, on each side dash
The splintered ice with thundering crash ;
A fragment strikes him ; ha ! he reels ;
That shock in every nerve he feels ;
Faster, bold raftman, speed thy way,

The waves roar round thee for their prey;
The cabin totters, — sinks, — the flood
Rolls its mad surges where it stood:
Before thy straining sight, the hill
Sleeps in the moonlight, bright and still.
Falter not, falter not, struggle on,
That goal of safety may be won;
Heavily droops thy wife with fear,
Thy boy's shrill shriekings fill thine ear;
Urge, urge thy strength to where out-fling
Yon cedar branches for thy cling.
Joy, raftman, joy! thy need is past,
The wished-for goal is won at last.
Joy, raftman, joy! thy quick foot now
Is resting on the upland's brow.
Praise to high Heaven! each knee is bent,
And every heart in prayer of grateful love is blent.

ONNAWAH.

Away from Man's close haunts, his toils and cares,
And mean ambitions. In the deepest core
Of the free wilderness, a crystal sheet
Expands its mirror to the trees that crowd
Its sloping borders. Oft in life's green spring
My foot hath wandered to its lovely side,
That Nature's purity might cleanse my heart
From stains of human contact, as a wind
Clears from the sky its clouds.
A morn in June.
A hood of gray is o'er. The waters sleep, —
A plain of glass. Through the thick, heavy air
Far echoes ring. A dampness slight, that steals
Across the brow, foretells the misty rain
From the cold east. With swift and gladsome step
I bend my way to where upon a bank
Stands a rude hut of logs. Black stumps are round,
The red-stemmed buckwheat struggling up between,
And the bright rye slim lengthening into stalks.
Here dwells an aged hermit of the wild.
His keen black eye and tinted skin proclaim
An Indian fountain to his blood, and taught
By Nature only, here his days have passed.

His linden-scooped canoe is launched, and forth
We glide upon the lake. Each paddle-dash
Wakens an echo. Quick the slender pike
Shoots from the surface like a scaly dart,
His splashing fall loud smiting on the ear.
Light breaking bubbles tell of finny sports
On every hand, while in the mottled depths
Along the side of our canoe, dark backs
Glance like swift phantoms. Off a long low point
Without the net of lily-stems, we drop
The anchoring stone, and through the light-winged hours
We ply our sport. The sunset glows, and then,
As wearied we recline, the old man tells
The legend of the lake.

"Long years ago,
An aged Indian with his only son
Dwelt in yon hut,—the last of that great tribe
Which kindled once their fires upon the spot
Where the twin branches of the Delaware
Glide into one, and in their language called
Chihocken, or the Meeting of the Floods.
Bright was this lake to gray-haired Onnawah,
As those pure waters that the mind oft sees
In the far spirit-land. The old bald pines
Stood for his fathers; in the winds he heard
The voice of her long perished, and the flowers
Seemed smiling with his children's merry looks;
His son, I say, was all that now remained
Of his once crowded lodge.

One Autumn morn
That son departed on a distant hunt.
With broken rifle-lock he homeward bent
His steps, and now upon a hill he paused
To rest him from his toil. Beneath him lay
The placid lake, so near, the fanning wind
Could waft his lightest crest-plume on its face.
In the blue western smoke the beamless sun
Was plunging, and the red tints of the lake
Were paling into gray. Off this same point
The sire was seated in his bark canoe,
Luring the hungry pike. The old man's form
Was touched by one slant ray that melted off
Even as the son gazed on him. Sweet and still
The peaceful scene, as though the holy smile
Of the Great Spirit hallowed it. The son
Felt his heart swell, and low he knelt to bless
His Manitou that he had still a sire.
Hark! a sharp cracking sound! a rifle-shot
From the twined shore below. He started up.
His sire had fallen with breast athwart the side
Of the down-slanted bark; a tinge of blood
Was on the glassy water. With a shout
Of taunting triumph, forth a figure sprang
From a deep thicket. At one glance the son
That figure knew, — a pale-face who had lost
The inmates of his hearth by one fierce sweep
Of torch and tomahawk, but wielded not
By those who had a kindred drop in veins
Of sire or son; no, no, — I swear it, youth,

By the Great Spirit. But the pale-face vowed,
Vowed to his God his stern revenge should seek
All, all of Indian race. The son, I say,
Knew the quick leaping form, and down he dashed
With heart all flame, and feet like darting wings.
The ruthless murderer had plunged within
The ruffled water, and I — he — the son
Leaped in his rippling track. His hand had touched
The sacred head of my — the sire, with knife
Keen for the scalp; but now the son was there.
With one strong grasp I tore him from his hold,
And clutched his throat; twice, twice I felt the thrill
Of his cold piercing knife, but in that grasp
My strength was centred. Out his eyeballs strained:
Ha! ha! black grew his swelling features, forth
His quivering tongue was thrust: ha! ha! his form
Writhed like a snake's. With one hand then I seized
His streaming hair, as I this lock, and bent
The head down deep within the splashing waves,
Till shudderings shook no more his nerveless frame,
And the quick globules no more gurgled up
To the red surface. Loosened from my clutch,
Drooping, he sank, while to the rocking side
Of the canoe that held the father's form,
The son — youth, have I said 't was I! — then clung,
And climbed, though fainting with his wounds, within.
The point was near, and with his precious load
He slowly won his way, till o'er the sand
He dragged, with staggering steps, his stiffening sire,
And placed him in a pit an upturned pine

Had hollowed; heaped the form with withered leaves,
And then sank down to die. But not so willed
Had the Great Spirit. A young hunter found
The bleeding form, bound up the wounds, and bore
The sufferer to the hut, and o'er him watched,
Till life again ran freely in his veins.
When he arose, within a fitting grave
He placed his sire. Youth, seest thou yon green
mound,
O'er which the laurel hangs its chalice-flowers?
There sits gray Onnawah, with calumet
And knife and hatchet, waiting till the son
Shall join him, and together they begin
Their brierless journey to the spirit-land."

THE HUNTER'S FLIGHT.

SULTRY and close was the noontide air!
The fire of August was burning there.
No cloud sent shade, and no wind breathed sigh,
To the thirsty earth, through the brassy sky;
Even drooped, in the depths of the forest bowers,
The shrivelling leaves and the shrinking flowers:
And faintly, and slowly, the hunter strode
By the blaze-tree and moss of his lonely road.

He saw, as he looked through his narrow bound,
But a red haze mantling each object around,
So thick, that his footfall nearly trod
On the black snake basking along the sod,
And touched with his rifle the rabbit that crouched
More close in the bush where it tremblingly couched;
The gossamer motionless hung from the spray
Where the weight of the dew-drop had torn it away;
The rock, by the aspen, stood not more still
Than those delicate leaves an air-whisper could thrill;
And the seed of the thistle, that whisper could swing
Aloft on its wheel, as though borne on a wing
When the yellow-bird severed it, dipping across,

Its soft plumes unruffled, fell down to the moss.
The foot of the hunter sunk deep in the mass
Of green slime, which late gushed a clear brook,
through the grass ;
And on, as he struggled, his breath came thick,
And his limbs turned faint, and his spirit sick.

Upon a prostrate, mossy trunk,
At length the toil-worn hunter sunk.
The insect's whirring clarion wound
Up from the grass, with lulling sound;
The quail's quick whistle echoed clear
From the red buckwheat-stubble near ;
The drowsy murmur of the bee,
The bird's low twitter from the tree,
His beating pulses soothed, till sleep
Stole on his eyelids, sweet and deep.

Dreams hold their empire now :
In the cool stream his lip is revelling deep,
Round his hot skin the balmy breezes creep,
Until the clammy hair sits lightly on his brow.

Now on the mountain ledge
With his fleet hound, he tracks the flying deer ;
And now, with its loud thunders in his ear,
He sends his skimming bark along the torrent's
edge.

More loudly swelled the torrent's sound,

It seemed to fill the air around,
And wakening with a start of fear,
That deep, stern roar still met his ear;
Thick stifling smoke obscured his view
With fiery spots fierce glaring through;
Up a near summit sped his flight,
There burst the scene upon his sight.

An ocean of flame far was blazing and roaring,
And, whirling and surging, swift onward was pouring;
The forest was rocking and plunging below
In a gulf, which each fall made more fiercely to glow;
The tallest trees melted away like a breath
As those waves circled on, full of horror and death;
And the ground seemed to crumble, while high over all
Dense, black, and gigantic, smoke hung like a pall.
As onward this cataract awful careered,
The scene to the terrified hunter appeared
Like a demon aroused, marching on in his ire,
With trumpet of thunder and banner of fire.

An instant gazed the hunter there,
The instant whelmed in deep despair.
Then bounding, he flew on his footstep of wind
From the flames, that more fiercely came rolling behind.
Red gleams were darting o'er his head;
Like rain, the coals were round him shed,

And a huge pine beside him thundered,
Blinding his sight with fragments sundered.
As swifter speeds he, winged with fear,
Hark! piercing howls come swelling near.
With jaw of foam, and skin scorched black,
And rolling eye, and bristling back,
Tearing his flesh with pain and wrath,
A panther bounds along his path.

But now, quick silvery sparkles break
Upon his eye: the lake — the lake —
Bursts to his view; oh! cool and sweet
The waters gurgle at his feet:
One plunge in their crystal — the hunter laves
His feverish limbs in the laughing waves,
And he cleaves his way to the refuge before,
Where the forest stands green on the opposite shore.

On the moist soft verdure the hunter bends,
His incense of thanks for his safety ascends.
To the brink of the lake yawns the red abyss,
Like serpents the flames on its edges hiss;
But a gleam flashed o'er, more quick and keen
Than the dart of the blaze in that burning scene,
And a sound rolled by, more stern and deep
Than the roar of that element's wildest sweep;
The frowning storm-cloud's voice and eye
Spreading his mantle across the sky.
In thick gray sheets poured the drenching rain,
And the flames shrank back with their greedy train,

Now cowering low, and now flashing high
With a fitful start, to sink down and die.
Still more fierce and more fast dashed the rain, till attired
In his shroud of thick smoke, the red Demon expired.

INDIAN CORN.

When the warm sunshine and the southern wind
Have tinged the russet of the basking hills,
And made warm sheltered nooks grow hourly green,—
When buds swell on the boughs, and under banks,
The eye is sweetly startled by the sight
Of the white violet, where, the day before,
Its slender stem was hidden in the moss,—
Come to the field where swift the rich dark soil
Is curling into ridges, as the share
Glides on its way. The tawny furrows now
Fill the wide space. The yellow seeds are dropped,
And the soft, earth is loosly mounded o'er.
Sun-gleams and rain-streaks braided, hourly give
Their generous influence. Once more to the field.
Points of deep green are bristling on their hills,—
The infant plants. Each day rears up the shoots.
Now cawings fill the air, as from the wood
The thievish flock, swift flying, stoops below ;
And then black shapes are scattered in the green,
Strutting and croaking, busily tearing up
The tender roots, while slow along the fence
The stealing farmer with his ready gun
Scans keen his hoped-for prey. But lo ! a croak

From some high rail, and on broad skimming wing
Darts the whole flock, with guttural chorus, off,
Just as the gun is aiming. Next the dawn
Falls gray and indistinct, upon a shape
Gaudily decked within the cornfield's midst,
Nodding its limbs to every breath of air.
The crow commander, from the hemlock's top,
Eyes the strange form askance; from greater height
Still looks, and as the object yet remains,
Leads off his legions to the neighboring field.
But now the tall, slim stalks put forth long leaves,
And while the summer brightens to its prime,
Their heads are tipped with plumes, and from their sides,
Fringes of yellow silk and long green cones
Proclaim the swelling ears. The burning sun
Pours down its withering fire, and up the stalks
Still rise, the fringes deepen, and the ears
Grow rounder, while the buckwheat in the heat
Shrivels and blackens.
Opal Autumn comes.
The tops are sever'd, and the crackling sheaths
Show, through the frequent rents, the thick-set grains
Glazed into flinty gold. A few more days,
And then brown stacks, the stubble spotting, tell
The labor of the reaper. Soon the barn
Groans with the toil-won treasures. When the blasts
Of chill November warn that Winter, stern
And fierce, is on his way, and fitfully
Snow specks the harsh gray air, the freezing Night,

Stiffening the frame of nature, knits anew
The social ties within the kitchen walls,
Kindled by the red tongue that fills the jaws
Of the huge fireplace, with the ruddy gleams,
Dancing on flitches from the rafters hung, —
On pumpkins ranged in rows along the floor,
And on the pile of maize ears; merrily
The husking group of youths and maidens ply
Their sportive toil, loud laughing, as the jest
Flies lightly round; while with a placid smile
Old age looks on, and in its happiest glee,
Childhood sports round, pursuing now with shouts
The frisking kitten, doubling up the ears
Of the old crouching dog, or seeing through
The window-pane the crimson phantom face
Quivering upon the gloom without, awe-struck
Into brief silence. Thus the hours pass by,
Until the music of the violin
Tells that the work is o'er, the dance begun.
Then jolts the heavy wagon o'er the road,
To the red mill, heaped up with rounded bags,
And soon the golden flour pours warm from out
The busy hopper. Now the precious grain
Performs its grateful office: food for man,
It lights the winter hearth with cheerfulness,
Gladdens the heart, and causes it to raise
Thanksgivings to the Holy One who grants
Seed-time and harvest to His footstool earth.

SKATING.

THE thaw came on with its southern wind
  And misty drizzly rain ;
The hill-side showed its russet dress,
  Dark runnels seamed the plain ;
The snowdrifts melted off like breath,
  The forest dropped its load,
The lake, instead of its mantle white,
  A liquid mirror showed ;
It seemed — so soft was the brooding fog,
  So fanning was the breeze —
You 'd meet with violets in the grass
  And blossoms on the trees.

But shortly before the sundown,
  The gray and spongy clouds
Began to break above the head
  And hurry away in crowds ;
The bland wind shifted to the west,
  Where a stripe of brassy light
Glowed like the flame of a furnace,
  When the sun had passed from sight ;
And, in the fleeting twilight, cold
  And colder waxed the air,

Till it fell on the brow like the touch of ice,
  As the still night darkened there.

Oh, bitter were the hours ! and those
  Who, wakeful, marked them pass,
Could hear the snap of table and chair
  And ring of breaking glass ;
Without, though the wind was quiet,
  Crack, crack, went the maple and oak,
As if some mighty trampling power
  Those huge stems downward broke ;
The very wolf, the fierce, gaunt wolf,
  Though famishing, to his cave
Crept shivering back, nor sought again,
  The deadly cold to brave.

And morning glowed with a heartless sun
  And a heaven of harshest blue,
And an air that pricked and stung the skin,
  As if darts invisible flew ;
But oh the sight, the radiant sight
  That broke upon the eye !
Millions of sparkles danced around
  Of every varied dye ;
The boughs were steel, the roofs were steel,
  With icicles hanging down,
Steel gave a helmet to the hill, —
  To the mountain-top a crown.

The lake, far, far, it stretched, no gem
  More pure, more clear and bright ;

Solid as iron, and smooth as glass,
  It froze in a single night;
When sunk the sun, 't was a watery waste,
  With ripples upon its gloss;
When rose the sun, 't was a polished plain
  That a steed might safely cross;
How free would glide the skate now:
  Hurrah for a pleasant day!
To the lake-side, to the lake-side,
  Away, my boys, away.

We bind our feet with their steely wings,
  And we launch along in glee;
Hurrah, hurrah, how swift we go!
  No bird more swift than we;
We hiss along our glittering path,
  The banks slide quickly by,
The trees within spin round and round,
  And above is a gliding sky;
The eagle is fleet, but we envy him not,
  Though all heaven is his domain,
He cannot feel more eager joy
  Than we on this glassy plain.

Beneath us glares the mottled ice
  With great white clefts athwart,
Broke by the lake in its toil to breathe;
  Hark now to the sharp report!
What a rumble is passing all over,
  A groan so hollow and deep,

Surely the lake is rent in twain :
  The heart gives fearful leap.
No, no, as well might the diamond break
  When ringing to a blow.
Hurrah ! then onward, onward, boys,
  More swift, more merrily go.

Our shadows gleam before our track,
  The air hums in our ears, —
The pure clear air, the mountain air,
  How it braces, how it cheers !
We cluster in groups, we scatter away,
  We whirl, we rush, we wheel, —
All round us are figures of strange device
  Engraved by the flashing steel ;
Again that dismal bellow !
  How the prisoned lake roars out !
But it cannot burst from its manacle,
  For all its angry shout.

Ha ! why do the foremost in yon race
  Upon their heels lean back ?
The ground ice flies from their skates like froth,
  As they stop in their deep-cut track ;
We all approach : 't is a little space
  The lake has burst for air,
Spread o'er with a film like isinglass ;
  Back, back, for death is there !
The miller's boy one year ago,
  Rushed swift on a spot like this ;

One crack of the brittle ice, one shriek,
And he sank in the abyss.

Oh quickly we hurried toward the place,
With deadly fear and awe ;
Afar in the freezing element
His struggling form we saw :
Oh quickly all hurried with might and main,
For we knew he could not swim,
But ere the fleetest could reach the spot,
No aid was there for him ;
We saw his blue and ghastly face
Sink down in the rippling flood,
And then we gazed on the empty space
With horror-frozen blood.

But by-and-by his father came
With pale and frenzied look,
He reached the border of the space,
And then one leap he took ;
One leap he took, and the waters closed
In whirls above his head,
A moment, and he rose to view,
And with him rose the dead, —
The dead all drooping and crusted o'er
With particles of frost, —
And the strong man, weeping, bore away
His only and his lost.

We leave the spot : to the outlet bank
We glide for an instant's rest,

This log, edged round with crystals, yields
  A seat upon its breast ;
Our tight-bound feet are aching,
  But our veins glow warm and free ;
Ha, ha ! in that hollow of weak white ice,
  Joe tumbles to his knee !
But look to the icy lace-work
  Embroidered around the bank !
And see, how the frozen rushes stand
  In sparkling jewelled rank !

Again away : but the sun has sunk,
  And the west, — what a gorgeous view !
An orange base, red, green, and gray,
  Thence deepening up to blue ;
And now, low flying to their woods,
  Those distant crows, whose caws
Have faintly touched the ear, are lost,
  As closer the twilight draws ;
And now dark night, dark starry night,
  For it is but a brief delay
From the golden tip of the loftiest pine
  To the arch of the milky way.

Dark night, dark starry night, and above
  How bright the clusters glow !
Here steadily burning orbs, and there
  One sheet of twinkling snow.
The bank is a mass of frowning gloom,
  And the ice just gives to view

A few star glimmerings at our feet,
  Then shrinks in darkness too.
But what care we for the darkness,
  For the shallows of the lake
Are spotted round with stumps, and there
  Our bonfires will we wake.

Red sparkles dance from the smitten steel,
  On the leaves and sticks we heap ;
Hurrah ! what glorious pyramids
  Of clear flame upward leap !
What a flashing glow is shed about !
  The ice, in crimson, gleams,
And the dark woods of the outlet
  Are kindled by the beams ;
So bare start out their depths to sight,
  That the moss of the old dead pines
Down hanging in flakes from the topmost limbs,
  Like golden network shines.

Hark to those fierce but lessening snarls !
  We have frightened some wolf away,
Some prowling wolf, this freezing night
  On the lookout for his prey ;
Again : a crash in the forest limbs,
  A panther's startled spring;
From the deepest haunt of the wilderness
  His keen shriek soon will ring ;
In the magic circle of this light
  We fear no forest-foe ;

Hurrah ! hurrah ! o'er the blushing ice
  We merrily, merrily go !

But the hours are wearing into the night,
  Our limbs are in need of rest,
And hark ! shrill rushing down the lake
  Comes a gust from the dread northwest ;
'T is the first breath of the tempest,
  And mark ! in the spangled sky,
Like surges of a gloomy sea,
  Shoot clouds of murkiest dye.
'T will be a wild, wild winter night
  Of bitter hail and sleet,
But within the walls of our happy homes
  We 'll slumber sound and sweet.

AN AUTUMN LANDSCAPE.

A SLOPE of upland, shorn by nibbling sheep
To a rich carpet, woven of short grass
And tiny clover, upward leads my steps
By the seamed pathway, and my roving eye
Drinks in the vassal landscape. Far and wide
Nature is smiling in her loveliness.
Masses of woods, green strips of fields, ravines
Shown by their outlines drawn against the hills,
Chimneys and roofs, trees, single and in groups,
Bright curves of brooks, and vanishing mountain-tops
Expand upon my sight. October's brush
The scene has colored; not with those broad hues
Mixed in his later palette by the frost,
And dashed upon the picture till the eye
Aches with the varied splendor, but in tints
Left by light scattered touches. Overhead
There shines a blending of cloud, haze, and sky
A silvery sheet with spaces of soft blue;
A trembling veil of gauze is stretched athwart
The shadowy hill-sides and dark forest-flanks;
A soothing quiet broods upon the air,

And the faint sunshine winks with drowsiness.
Far sounds melt mellow on the ear : the bark —
The bleat — the tinkle — whistle — blast of horn —
The rattle of the wagon-wheel — the low —
The fowler's shot — the twitter of the bird,
And even the hum of converse from the road.
The grass, with its low insect-tones, appears
As murmuring in its sleep. This butterfly
Seems as if loath to stir, so lazily
It flutters by. In fitful starts and stops
The locust sings. The grasshopper breaks out
In brief harsh strains amid its pausing chirps ;
The beetle, glistening in its sable mail,
Slow climbs the clover-tops, and even the ant
Darts round less eagerly.
What difference marks
The scene from yester-noontide. Then the sky
Showed such rich, tender blue, it seemed as if
'T would melt before the sight. The glittering clouds
Floated above, the trees danced glad below
To the fresh wind. The sunshine flashed on streams,
Sparkled on leaves, and laughed on fields and woods.
All, all was life and motion, as all now
Is sleep and quiet. Nature in her change
Varies each day, as in the world of man
She moulds the differing features. Yea, each leaf
Is variant from its fellow. Yet her works
Are blended in a glorious harmony,
For thus God made His earth. Perchance His breath

Was music when he spake it into life,
Adding thereby another instrument
To the innumerable choral orbs
Sending the tribute of their grateful praise
In ceaseless anthems toward His sacred throne.

THE SETTLER.

HIS echoing axe the settler swung
  Amid the sealike solitude,
And rushing, thundering, down were flung
  The Titans of the wood ;
Loud shrieked the eagle as he dashed
From out his mossy nest, which crashed
  Beneath the conquering blow,
And the first sunlight, leaping, flashed
  On the wolf's haunt below.

Rude was the garb, and strong the frame
  Of him who plied his ceaseless toil :
To form that garb, the wild-wood game
  Contributed their spoil ;
The soul that warmed that frame, disdained
The tinsel, gaud, and glare, that reigned
  Where men their crowds collect ;
The simple fur, untrimmed, unstained,
  This forest-tamer decked.

The paths which wound mid gorgeous trees,
  The streams whose bright lips kissed their flowers,
The winds that swelled their harmonies
  Through those sun-hiding bowers,

The brown ravine — the green arcade,
The nestling vale — the grassy glade,
  In woods all round unfurled,
These scenes and sounds majestic, made
  His lonely, only world.

His roof adorned a lovely spot,
  Mid the black logs green glowed the grain,
And many a plant the woods knew not,
  Throve in the sun and rain.
The smoke-wreath curling o'er the dell,
The low — the bleat — the tinkling bell,
  All made a landscape strange,
Which was the living chronicle
  Of deeds that wrought the change.

The violet smiled at spring's first tinge,
  The rose of summer spread its glow,
The maize hung out its autumn fringe,
  Rude winter brought its snow;
And still the settler labored there,
His shout and whistle woke the air,
  As cheerily he plied
His garden-spade, or drove his share
  Along the hillock's side.

He marked the fire-storm's blazing flood
  Roaring and crackling on its path,
And scorching earth, and melting wood,
  Beneath its greedy wrath;

He marked the rapid whirlwind shoot
Trampling the pine-tree with its foot,
  And darkening thick the day
With streaming bough and severed root,
  Hurled whizzing on its way.

His gaunt hound yelled, his rifle flashed,
  The grim bear hushed its savage growl,
In blood and foam the panther gnashed
  Its fangs, with dying howl;
The fleet deer ceased its flying bound,
Its snarling wolf-foe bit the ground,
  And with its moaning cry
The beaver sank beneath the wound,
  Its pond-built Venice by.

Humble the lot, yet his the race!
  When Liberty sent forth her cry,
Who thronged in Conflict's deadliest place,
  To fight — to bleed — to die.
Who cumbered Bunker's height of red,
By hope, through weary years were led,
  And witnessed Yorktown's sun
Blaze on a Nation's banner spread,
  A Nation's freedom won.

THE PINE-TREE.

STERN dweller of the mountain ! with thy feet
Grasping the crag, and lifting to the sky
Thy haughty crest ! Stern warrior king ! thy form
Scarce deigns to shake, when even the mighty blast
Which the strong eagle fears to stem, swoops down
And breaks upon thee. O'er the glimmering chasm
As leanest thou, with one giant limb outspread
Thy sceptre, and seamed armor on thy breast,
What is more grand, more glorious than thou !
The headlong torrent pitching at thy base
Sends forth but vassal rumblings, when the storm
Awakes thy thunder, and the puny woods
Seem like bent saplings when thy towering shape
Swings in its majesty. The lightning's dart
Hath streaked, but not consumed thee : upward still
As the black chariot of the fiend o'er rolls,
Upward still, warrior-king, thy crest doth point,
And in sublime defiance dost thou fling
Thy emerald robe from off thy wounded breast,
For other blows to fall, fierce hissing forth
Thy scorn as flies the tempest. On thy rock,
Thy throne impregnable, thou hast not reigned
During the lapse of ages, for a blast

To break thee, nor a lightning-shaft to cleave
Thy plumed head to the earth. The hurricane
And showers of blazing levin-bolts alone
Can hurl thee from thy post of centuries.

Yet art thou gentle, monarch of the crag!
When all is gentle round thee: when the sky
Is soft with summer, and the sunshine basks
In love upon thy branches, bright-winged birds
Flutter within thy plumes, and make thee gay
With their sweet songs: the downy-pinioned breeze
Soothes thee, until thou murmurest in a voice
Of blandest music, that upon the ear
Steals like a long-drawn sigh.

As proud thy head
Bears the wild tempest when its rains are launched
In slanted phalanx, so when from the west
The wind fans lightly, and the parted clouds
Let the fresh sunshine leap, thy branches drop
Their sprinklings on the blossom hung beneath,
Till its blue eye shines deeper in its blue,
And floats its sweet breath sweeter, while the moss
That plump and green o'erspread thy iron roots,
Fringed delicate sandals, seem some trysting-place,
Where fairy shapes of gold and ebony
Glance o'er in mazy dances. Winter bleak,
Howling through forests changed to skeletons
At the first mimicking breath of Autumn sent.
As the mere Courier of his dread approach,

Though hurling all his blasts, from thee recoils,
His fury spent in vain: not one slight plume,
No, not the tiniest fibre of thy sprays
Blanches or falls; but as thou stoodest when Spring
Made earth leap living at the bluebird call,
Unchanged wilt thou again her carol hail,
And tell where passed her timid steps from prints
Of violets and of cowslips.
Let us mark,
Proud pine! thou one of myriad instruments
Through which mysterious solemn Nature breathes
The music of her wisdom in our souls;
Oh let us mark thy likeness in the world,
The wondrous world of man. True Greatness towers
A glorious monarch, throned on craggy thought
Decked in its proud regalia. When the blast
Of Fortune bursts, it bends not: o'er the herd
It spreads its sceptred arm, and weaker souls
Bow, when occasion wakes its energies
In all their native glory. Earth's wild storms
May sweep across it, and their lightnings touch
Its lifted crest, but haughtily it dares
The scathing wrath, and casts its deepest scorn
At the endeavor baffled. Glorious gifts
Are not bestowed for every passing cloud
Of life to lay them darkened in the dust.

And it is gentle too, when gentle hearts
Are round it; love for love it freely gives,
And while it bears the storm upon its head,

It yields a cherishing care to those that cling
Unto it for protection. In life's change
It changes not, but as it smiled in joy,
So in the bleak waste of adversity,
It wears its customed look, and welcomes back
The sunshine of renewed prosperity.

THE INDIAN'S VIGIL.

The untouched forest depth displayed
Its thick, rich roof of summer shade,
  With sunshine streaming broad across,
Bathing the hemlock's sloping top,
And showering mid the elm, to drop
  In golden spots upon the moss;
Or, slanting through green clefts, to pass
In narrow streaks along the grass
  Of some wild tree-notched road
Whose leafy fretwork, arching high,
Glimpses of cloud, and dots of sky,
  The upward vision showed.

Here reared the beech its sprinkled bark
Beside the maple's rough and dark,
  And birchen column smooth and gray;
There, prostrate on its place of birth,
Raising its mass of clinging earth,
  The wind-fallen woodland giant lay.
Where, grasping with its knotted wreath
Of roots, the moundlike trunk, beneath
  In brown wet fragments spread,
A young usurping sapling reigned,

Nature, Mezentius-like, had chained
  The living with the dead.

Within the deepest of the wood,
Where the huge bolls more scattering stood,
  An area lay of grass and flowers ;
There the blue violet modestly
Shrank from the murmuring kissing bee,
  And sweetly in the bordering bowers
His changing notes the thrasher sung,
While the gray squirrel's chatterings rung
  At each spray-bending bound.
And tapping up the mossy oak
The checkered flicker also woke
  The sylvan echoes round.

An eagle, in this lovely scene,
Stood perched upon a hillock green,
  Where strewed remains of bow and spear
With here and there a scattered bone,
Bared by the frost and rain, made known
  An Indian burial-place was here.
And as he stood, his form stretched high,
And from his keen and martial eye
  Glances around he shot,
He seemed, within the halo-light
With ruffled plumes, and crown of white,
  The monarch of the spot.

Balancing on his outspread wing,
  At length he looked as if to spring,

While higher arched his kingly neck ;
Rustled the leaves, and with a shriek
He swept up, pointing high his beak,
And dwindled to a fading speck.
The next, an Indian from the wood,
Stepped in that scene of solitude
And knelt before the mound,
With kindling eye and solemn air,
As though, at last, its Mecca there
His pilgrimage had found.

Worn were his moccasins, — his trail
From where the Rocky Mountains' gale
Ruffles Missouri's farthest source,
Where herds the bison, prowls the bear,
And wild horse snuffs the prairie air
And scours along his curbless course.
He, by a deathless wish impelled
To view the sacred mound, which held
The ashes of his race,
Earth-blended remnants, — yet that made
This lone, green, forest-nestling glade
A consecrated place.

Now wafted by the west wind's sigh
A gray cloud stole across the sky,
The pleasant shower that summer weaves,
And, with the streaming sunshine blent,
Its fine and gentle droppings sent
In pattering music on the leaves.

It lifted, and the wind, bequeathed
With the fresh forest-odors, breathed
From every verdant thing, —
The birch, the spruce, the sassafras,
The fern, the pine, the moss, the grass, —
Crept on with burdened wing.

Sunset, with all its opal hues,
Glowed, faded, with the melting dews,
And o'er the cedar's tapering height
The young moon bent her brightening bow
And cast her deepening gleams below,
As twilight darkened into night.
Timidly from the pearly sky,
Opened each star its sparkling eye,
Then, red the crescent sank,
And fire-flies, through the gloom that lowered,
Their fitful golden spangles showered
About the outlined bank.

The myriad sounds the ear heeds not
When sunshine glows — now filled the spot;
The streamlet spoke in purling flow,
Murmured the leaves, — the spider's clock
Ticked in some crevice of the rock,
Blent with the cricket's chirping low.
While frequent, from the slimy bog
Came the hoarse bugle of the frog
And night-hawk's downward rush;
And every brooding pause to fill

The tree-toad's sweet continuous trill
  Swelled through this breathing hush.

What were the thoughts that o'er him swept,
As there the lone one vigil kept?
  Did not the bones that filled the mound
Shaped into forms, arise anew,
And gather to his mental view
  Instinct with life, above — around!
The fathers at their council-fire,
The warriors in their battle-ire,
  The maidens true and fair;
And one with fawnlike step and eye,
He thought she was too young to die,
  Was she too smiling there?

And morning came; the pure cool breeze
Brought rustling leaf-tones from the trees,
  Night's purple changed to crimson sheen;
The stars shrank back — the vapors white,
That webbed the branches, took their flight,
  And bursts of warblings woke the scene.
The deer stole timorous to the brook,
Its drumming wing the partridge shook,
  The darting sunbeams glowed;
And sadly from his musing bed,
The faithful Indian rose, to tread
  Again his homeward road.

Emerging from the forest dim,
There lay a bitter scene to him.

Gardens, and fields, and village spires,
And human groups; he heard the air
Ring with the axe; he saw the share
Tearing the earth; the fallow fires
Eating the trees. He fiercely turned,
And the soiled earth beneath him spurned;
And ne'er, mid waving grain
And thickening roofs, the Indian found
That glassy glade, — that hallowed mound,
His nation's tomb, again.

THE HARMONY OF THE UNIVERSE.

God made the world in perfect harmony.
Earth, air, and water, in its order, each
With its innumerable links, compose
But one unbroken chain; the human soul
The clasp that binds it to His mighty arm.

A sympathy throughout each order reigns.
A touch upon one link is felt by all
Its kindred, and the influence ceaseth not
Forever. The massed atoms of the earth,
Jarred by the rending of its quivering breast,
Carry the movement in succession through
To the extremest bounds, so that the foot,
Tracking the regions of eternal frost,
Unknowing, treads upon a soil that throbs
With the equator's earthquake.
The tall oak,
Thundering its fall in Apalachian woods,
Though the stern echo on the ear is lost,
Displaces, with its groan, the rings of air,
Until the swift and subtle messengers
Bear, each from each, the undulations on
To the rich palace of eternal Spring

That smiles upon the Ganges. Yea, on pass
The quick vibrations through the airy realms,
Not lost, until with Time's last gasp they die.

The craggy iceberg rocking o'er the surge,
Telling its pathway by its crashing bolts,
Strikes its keen teeth within the shuddering bark,
When night frowns black. Down, headlong, shoots
the wreck,
Lost is the vortex in the dashing waves,
And the wild scene heaves wildly as before;
But every particle that whirled and foamed
Above the groaning, plunging mass, hath urged
Its fellow, and the motion thus bequeathed
Lives in the ripple edging flowery slopes
With melting lace-work; or with dimples rings
Smooth basins, where the hanging orange-branch
Showers fragrant snow, and then it ruffles on,
Until it sinks upon Eternity.

Thus naught is lost in that harmonious chain,
That, changing momently, is perfect still.
God, whose drawn breaths are ages, with those
breaths
Renews its lustre. So 't will ever be,
Till, with one wave of His majestic arm,
He snaps the clasp away, and drops the chain
Again in chaos, shattered by its fall.

THE GARDEN.

WHEN the light flourish of the bluebird sounds,
And the south wind comes blandly; when the sky
Is soft in delicate blue with melting pearl
Spotting its bosom, all proclaiming Spring,
Oh with what joy the garden-spot we greet
Wakening from wintry slumbers. As we tread
The branching walks, within its hollowed nook,
We see the violet by some lingering flake
Of melting snow, its sweet eye lifting up
As welcoming our presence. Overhead
The fruit-tree buds are swelling, and we hail
Our grateful task of moulding into form
The waste around us. The quick delving spade
Upturns the fresh and odorous earth. The rake
Smooths the plump bed, and in their furrowed graves
We drop the seed. The robin stops his work
Upon the apple-bough, and flutters down,
Stealing, with oft-checked and uplifted foot,
And watchful gaze bent quickly either side,
Toward the fall'n wealth of food around the mouth
Of the light paper pouch upon the earth.
But fearful of our motions, off he flies,
And stoops upon the grub the spade has thrown

Loose from its den beside the wounded root.
Days pass along. The pattering shower falls down,
And then the warming sunshine. Tiny clefts
Tell that the seed has turned itself and swift
Is pushing up its stem. The fruit-trees now
Have broken into blossom; and the grape
Casting aside, in peels, its shrivelled skin,
Shows its soft furzy leaf of delicate pink;
And the thick midge-like blossoms round diffuse
A strong delicious fragrance. Soon along
The trellis stretch the tendrils, sharply pronged,
Clinging tenacious with their winding rings
And sending on the stem. A sheet of bloom
Then decks the garden, till the summer glows
Forming the perfect fruit. In showery nights
The fire-fly glances with its pendent lamp
Of greenish gold. Each dark nook owns a voice:
While perfume floats on every wave of air.
And as we reap the rich fruits of our toil
We bless the God who rains His gifts on us,
Making the earth its treasures rich to yield
With slight and fitful care. Our hearts should be
Ever but harps to send unceasing hymns
Of thankful praise to One who fills all space,
And yet looks down with smiles on lowly Man.

MORANNAH.

SUNBEAMS were glowing,
Streamlets were flowing,
Breezes were sweeping the beautiful sky;
But, contrast of sadness
To all this sweet gladness,
Morannah the chieftain was waiting to die.

Through a loop, a dart of flame
Shot by sunset, streaked the gloom;
Fired the prostrate warrior's frame,
Panther-robe and eagle-plume.
But the robe was stiff with gore,
Stained and bent the haughty crest;
Crimson drops were on floor,
Oozings of his mangled breast.

Round the block-house where he lay,
Sloped a knoll of green;
There the same slant sunset ray
Bathed a festive scene.
All the village throngs were there:
Aged men and children fair,
Hunters in their deerskin dress,

Just from out the wilderness;
Choppers with the glittering axe
Carried at their brawny backs;
All rejoicing o'er the fate
  Of that dying man,
Object long of fear and hate,
  Placed beneath a ban.

Fierce hunted like a wild beast, driven
  From wood to wood, from glen to glen,
Now climbing peaks by lightning riven,
  Now crouching in the panther's den,
Still roamed the forest-monarch free,
  Smiling disdain upon the foe,
Till deepest, foulest treachery,
  Brought the proud soaring eagle low.

Within the block-house walls, the morn
Had seen the hapless chieftain borne,
And now, the first white star of night
Would beam upon his spirit's flight.
The church's rude belfry, low, vane-topped, and square,
  And the octagon shape of the block-house, between,
Robed rich in the tints that are painted by air,
  The dome-rounded head of a mountain was seen.
There in the toil had the eagle been caught,
There was the deep damning treachery wrought.

That mountain's summit is a ledge;
  Upon each side a precipice

So sheer, each tree that grasps the edge
  Seems tottering o'er the deep abyss.
Oft had the chieftain found the place
A refuge from the white man's chase,
But the last warrior of his tribe
Had fallen before the proffered bribe ;
Tempted with gold, he had sworn to clear
The hunter's way to the slumbering deer.

Midst an oak's roots is a cavity
  Shelving down like a fox's den :
Standing beside the old gnarled tree,
  'T is hidden from the closest ken;
For long, thick fern-leaves there are hung,
An emerald veil o'er the entrance flung.
But the slant pit once passed, expand
  A cavern's walls, that, winding in,
Seem wrought out by a Titan's hand,
  The ledge's rocky heart to win.
On the dark passage leads, till high
Glimmers a faint glimpse of the sky
As through a cleft; the cavern ends,
But up a rough, wild stair ascends,
Scooped in the granite; till the tread
To the rock's towering height is led.

Midnight came with wind and cloud ;
      Now dark, now bright,
      The moon's rich light,
Fitfully glanced through the tattered shroud.

Through the gate of the palisade
Half a score of the settlers went
Just as the summer night begun,
(Half a score for the taking of one,)
Armed with rifle and with blade,
And swift their course to the mountain bent.
The gold-bought traitor at their head,
Up through the mountain woods they sped.
Skirting the precipice, threading the glen,
By the haunt of the wolf — near the rattlesnake's den;
Fierce eyeballs glared at them from tree and from nook,
The tempest in rage the dark wilderness shook;
Still, led by the guilty one, onward they wend,
To the lair of the guilty one's sachem and friend.

Now they are at the old oak-tree
Whose wreathed roots hide the cavity.
High above them soars the ledge,
Glimmering outlines mark the edge;
Naught they see, save here and there
Huge trees writhing in the air;
Naught they hear, save now and then
Wolf-howls from the neighboring glen;
While with fitful shriek and roar
Sweeps the wild wind, furious, o'er.

Down the little shelving hollow
Quick the wretched traitor slides;
One by one the settlers follow;
Slow along the cavern sides

Grope they onward, till the stair
Leads them to the upper air.

In a thicket's twining breast,
  Lies Morannah whelmed in sleep:
Chieftain, wake thee from thy rest!
  Foemen close around thee creep!
Closer, closer — wake, oh wake!
  Then, swift bounding from thy lair
Who thy foot could overtake
  Dashing down the rocky stair?
Baffled, known to none but thee,
  Clinging to the dangling grape,
To the slanting cedar-tree,
  Down the ledge — there leads escape.

Motionless, hapless Morannah lies,
  Closer and closer the foemen creep;
One more moment, they grasp their prize.
  Ha! a rustle! with startled leap
Up starts Morannah; in sudden sheen
Bursts the freed moonlight upon the scene.
It shows the crouching foe, and near,
Drawn back as if in mortal fear,
An Indian — what! his warrior there,
With trembling limbs and bristling hair!
Quick flashed the truth; his hatchet gleamed,
  Dead fell the traitor at his feet;
No more the fitful moonlight beamed,
  Away — away, his course is fleet;

A shot rings sharply on the night,
He staggers in his headlong flight;
Another brings him to his knee;
He rises, clinging to a bough,
And firmly braced against a tree,
He waits the foemen's coming now.
With his keen hatchet and his knife
Clutched tightly in his outstretched hands,
Ready to brave the unequal strife,
The bleeding forest-warrior stands.
As springs the panther from his lair,
His eyeballs flashing flames to dare,
Destruction's toils around him flung,
With one wild whoop, one sweeping blow,
Amid the back-recoiling foe
Morannah fiercely sprung.
And shrieking high his battle-yell,
He bleeding fought and fighting fell.

Still the low sunshine sweetly played
Upon the circling palisade;
It bathed with gold the knoll of green,
It streamed the village huts between;
The block-house on its western face
From steep projecting roof to base,
Was flooded with the radiance bright;
The loops seemed filled, like eyes, with light,
While the long ladder leaning there,
Stood pencilled sharply on the air.

Feebler grew Morannah's breath,
Keener grew the pain,
Phantoms, born of coming death,
Floated through his brain.
Phantoms of the stormy past
Thronging round him thick and fast, —
Till a single vision grew,
Living, to his mental view.

Where the deep woods their coverts spread,
Chasing the deer his steps were led,
And not till day its hazy course had run,
Bearing his spoils, his homeward course he won —
Ha! do his straining eyeballs see aright!
Where is the roof that met at morn his sight?
Where, oh where!
Naught but a black and smouldering waste is there:
All, all — his sire, his boy, his bride,
By white man's ruthless hands had died.
The tempest rose; in fiercest might
Through the surging forest bore,
And in that wild and fearful night
A bloody oath he swore,
While the lightning glared in sulphury light
And the thunder rattled o'er.

Another vision by him swept,
Well had that oath of blood been kept;
By day the field with carnage reeked,
At night the village sank in flame,

Until men bowed and women shrieked
  Where'er was spoke his name.

Then like the clouds in tempestuous strife,
By rolled the last closing scenes of his life.
The battle on the mountain's crest,
  Where, by a thousand foes hemmed round,
Striving to shield him with their breast
  A grave his faithful warriors found, —
His wounds, captivity, and flight,
  With his last tribesman by his side,
And then the scene of yesternight !
  Oh ! on that mountain had he died !
Then had no close walls choked his breath,
Hastening the wings of hovering death ;
His ear the taunt had never met,
The jest — the sneer — the epithet,
From those that shook in deadliest fear
  When night closed round its solemn shades,
Lest ere the day dawn they should hear
  His war-whoop round their palisades.

The sun now touched the horizon's rim ;
The slanting pickets faded dim ;
The block-house reared its rounded form,
Its roof yet tipped with radiance warm
Which melted off; but still the throng
Rejoiced in laughter and in song,
And not till night claimed earth and air,
Was the green block-house hillock bare.

As the first star gemmed twilight's gloom,
The hamlet's white-haired patriarch
Entered, with torch, the captive's room;
He heard a rattle in the dark.
Perchance he came to taunt the chief,
For the old man was fierce in ire;
Perchance he came to yield relief,
For age allays the spirit's fire.
He heard that rattle; high his torch he reared:
There lay the chieftain — there the warrior feared,
His limbs faint fluttering, while from out his throat
Came that death-rattle, — life's expiring note.
But as the light upon his brow was flung,
Up from his couch the dying sachem sprung, —
Up from his couch, and with one warrior look
In his clinched grasp his knife he feebly shook,
From his weak tongue one faltering war-whoop passed,
Then down the chieftain sank — death, death had come at last.

THE FALLS OF NORMAN'S KILL.[1]

A DAY in Indian Summer : here, the sky
Shows a bright veil of silver; there, a shade
Of soft and misty purple, with the fleece
Of downy clouds, and azure streaks between.
The light falls meekly, and the wooing air
Fans with a brisk vitality the frame.
The woods have lost the bright and varied charm
Of magic Autumn, and the faded leaves
Hide with one robe of brown the earth that late
Glowed like the fabled gardens of the East.
Still all around is lovely. Far the eye
Pierces the naked woods, and marks the shades,
Like prone black pillars with their capitals,
Formed by the sprays; and rocks, ravines, and mounds,
(Hidden when Summer smiles) and sparkling rills,
Trickling o'er mossy stones.
                                        A low, stern tone
Rumbles upon the air, as winding down
The gullied road, I seek the gorge where flows
The stream to mingle with the river flood

[1] The Norman's Kill is a stream about two miles south of Albany, the turnpike crossing it very near its entrance into the Hudson. The Falls are a little to the right, in a deep ravine.

In the brief eastward distance. On my left
Are the brown waters, a high rocky isle
Like a huge platform midway ; and the steep
Tree-columned ridge, in summer dense with shades,
But ragged now with gaunt and leafless boughs,
And only green where stand the kingly pines
And princely hemlocks. On my right the bank,
Of slate and crumbling gravel, pitches down
Now sheer, now hollowed out, the dark blue clay
Showing its strata veins, while on the edge
High up and dwarfed by distance, cling tall trees.
A rocky rampart, seamed and dashed with white,
Is piled before me, and the bending sky
Close at its back. Advancing, with the sound
Louder and louder, waters leap and gush
And foam through channelled outlets ; dashing now
O'er terraces, now flinging o'er a rock
A shifting fringe of silver, shooting quick
Through some deep gully, like a glassy dart,
And now in one rich mass of glittering foam
Sent downward, with light particles of spray
In white smoke rising.

Like the puny wrath
Of the weak child, to manhood's passion-burst
When his fierce heart is flaming ; like the voice
Of the low west wind, to the mighty sweep
Of the roused northern storm-blast, art thou now,
Oh rushing stream ! to when the roaring rains
Have swelled thy fountains, and with thundering shocks,
Foaming and leaping, thou dost dash along,

Restrainless in thy awful force, to rend
And whirl and whelm, until a mightier wave
Swallows thy raging being. Bridge and tree
Torn into fragments, roll and plunge and toss,
Till those that now might look on thee and smile,
Turn grave and tremble.
One more lesson deep
And sad, in Nature's ever opened book,
Art thou, bright stream! Change, quick and endless change,
Is ever moving round us. Sun and cloud,
Winter and summer, light and darkness, all,
All whirl their contrasts. Life may spread its path
Glorious with hope and beautiful with joy;
Home with its blessings, like an Eden smile;
Beware, gay, thoughtless dreamer! hush thy song!
Beware! Is joy immortal on the earth?
Beware! Hath angel Hope, with pointing hand
And buoyant pinion, never fled, and left
The fiend Despondency to fill her place
With blackness? Hush thy song, gay dreamer! pause
In thy light dancing tread! the awful change
May now, even now, be swift approaching thee.

THE SMITHY.

THERE crouched a little smithy at the corner of the road,
In the village where, when life shone fresh and bright, was my abode ;
A little slab-roofed smithy, of a stained and dusky red,
An ox-frame standing by the door, and at one side a shed ;
The road was lone and pleasant, with margins grassy-green,
Where browsing cows and nibbling geese from morn till night were seen.

High curled the smoke from the humble roof with dawning's earliest bird,
And the tinkle of the anvil, first of the village sounds, was heard ;
The bellows-puff, the hammer-beat, the whistle, and the song,
Told, steadfastly and merrily, toil rolled the hours along,
Till darkness fell, and the smithy then with its forge's clear deep light
Through chimney, window, door, and cleft, poured blushes on the night.

The morning shows its azure breast and scarf of silvery fleece,
The margin-grass is grouped with cows, and spotted o'er with geese ;
On the dew-wet green by the smithy, there 's a circle of crackling fire,
Hurrah ! how it blazes and curls around the coalman's welding tire !
While o'er it, with tongs, are the smith and his man, to fit it when cherry-red,
To the tilted wheel of the huge grimed ark in the background of the shed.

There 's a stony field on the ridge to plough, and Brindle must be shod,
And at noon, through the lane from the farm-house, I see him slowly plod ;
In the strong frame, chewing his cud, he patiently stands, but see !
The bands have been placed around him — he struggles to be free :
But John and Timothy hammer away, until each hoof is armed,
Then loosened Brindle looks all round, as if wondering he 's unharmed.

Joe Matson's horse wants shoeing, and at even-tide he 's seen,
An old gray sluggish creature, with his master on the green ;

Within the little smithy, old Dobbin, Matson draws,
There John is busily twisting screws, and Timothy filing saws;
The bellows sleeps, the forge is cold, and twilight dims the room,
With anvil, chain, and iron bar, faint glimmering through the gloom.

I stand beside the threshold and gaze upon the sight,
The doubtful shape of the old gray horse, and the points of glancing light:
But hark! the bellows wakens, out dance the sparks in air,
And now the forge is raked high up, now bursts it to a glare;
How brightly and how cheerily the sudden glow outbreaks,
And what a charming picture of the humble room it makes!

It glints upon the horseshoes on the ceiling-rafters hung,
On the anvil and the leaning sledge its quivering gleams are flung;
It touches with bronze the smith and his man, and it bathes old dozing gray,
And a blush is fixed on Matson's face in the broad and steady ray;
One moment more, and the iron is whirled with fierce and spattering glow,

And swank! swank! swank! rings the sledge's smite,
tink! tink! the hammer's blow.

"Whoe, Dobbin!" says Tim, as he pares the hoof,
"whoe! whoe!" as he fits the shoe,
And the clink of the driving nails is heard, till the
humble toil is through;
Pleased Matson mounts his old gray steed, and I hear
the heavy beat
Of the trotting hoofs up the corner road till the
sounds in the distance fleet;
And I depart with grateful joy to the King of earth
and heaven,
That even to life in its lowliest phase, such interest
should be given.

THE CAMP IN THE FOREST.

A BAND of hunters were we. All day long
Our feet had trailed the woods. The panther fierce,
The snorting bear, the cowering wolf, and deer
Swift as our balls, had fallen, as cracked the shots
Of our slim, deadly rifles. Sunset now
Was brightening the leaf-seas that swept all round,
As with a glory. In a lovely spot,
A little hollow glade, we stayed our steps.
Tempting it looked in pleasant grass, snowed o'er
With the white forest-clover. Scattered round
Were long, low, narrow mounds. Upon our brows
The delicate south wind broke, then melted smooth
Over each limb in balm. The western sky
Was made one glow with the descending sun,
Which, mid the mantling leaves and crowded trunks,
Showered bright and brilliant patches. The lone spot
Lay steeped in shade and coolness. From the stream
The low song of the ripples, as they purled
Over some knotted root, with now and then
The twitter of the snipe, sweet filled the air.
A sandy pathway, kindled rich and warm

By a slant beam, sloped downward to the lymph,
Through the thick alders. As the grateful wind
Poured its moist sweetness o'er our strengthening
frames,
We roused our camp-fire. From the bended boughs
We hung our spoil ; while on the ruddy coals
The broiling deer-flesh told of coming cheer.
Loud rose the talk and high the boast, and wide
The frequent song reëchoed, for the band
Though rude felt kindly. A gray light was spread
Across the hollow, but the tree-tops round
Cut sharp on mellow brightness. Deepest gold
Melting to rich transparent pearl, proclaimed
Where the blue-bosomed sun had disappeared.
Within the clefts of bushes, and beneath
The thickets, raven darkness frowned, but still
The leaves upon the edges of the trees
Preserved their shapes.
Our hunter cheer was past.
A glimmering dimness thickened in the air
Until the leaves were blended each in each.
The lurking darkness widened till it veiled
Thicket and bush. The neighboring throng of trunks
Retired within the gloom that hid the depths
Of the thick forest, till the brush of night
Had shaded in each object. Still a hue
Of brightness lingered round the tracery
Of the tree-summits, where a few pale stars
Were deepening ; while within the broad rich west
One orb — night's first — was beating like a pulse.

The camp-fire reared its crimson crackling cone,
Bronzing the dark, deep umbrage of the pine,
Spattering the thickets with great crimson blots,
And streaking, as with streams of blood, the sward.
So strong the ruddy gloss close round the fire,
The grass-blades twinkled, and the clover-tufts
Flashed out like silver spangles. In the depths
Of the black forest, where the gleams reached not,
The fire-flies sparkled, and within the nooks
The dead-wood showed a glaring like fierce eyes.
As the band sat around the camp-fire's glow,
The jest and song flew quickly ; legends strange
And stories of the woods, old daring feats,
Dangers escaped, and panther-fights, passed round
From lip to lip, till one old hunter, strong
And vigorous, though his form was gaunt and bent,
Glanced on the narrow mounds where flecks of gold
Had late been quivering, and with sorrowing voice
Told the dark, bloody legend of the spot.
" The hunters had been out, as we this day,
Beating the Willewemoc's woods, which then
Were far more lonely, wild, and dark than now.
Our village was a straggling hamlet, girt
With slanting palisades. As sunset glowed,
Our footsteps fell upon this self-same spot.
We halted. The melodious stream its gifts
Gave to our tongues. The golden-tinted woods
Laid on our brows their shadows, and the grass
Spread to our limbs its velvet. Song and tale,

As now, went round the group. High flashed our fire,
And the dark boughs blushed brightly in its glare.
Round the clear blaze the hunters stretched their frames,
Grasping their rifles. One — myself — was placed
As sentry to protect their helplessness.
The frog piped shrill its music, and the owl
Vied with the whippoorwill : all else was still.
Another hour, the fire had cowered below
Crouching and springing fitfully, and then
Licking the ashes. On my eyelids weighed
Sleep, heavily, like lead, while now and then
My brain would whirl in brief forgetfulness.
Hark! a twig snapped: hush! silence fell again,
'T was but a squirrel. Ha! from out the woods
Was not the blackness crawling in dim shapes
Near us? No, no, 't was but the glimmer of sleep
Within my fluttering eyelids. Still I heard
Each sylvan sound proclaiming peace and rest,
The owl-hoot, cricket-chirp, and sorrowing plaint
Of the lone whippoorwill, while myriad frogs
Rang out their silver chiming. Down I sank.
A burst of shrieks. The fire leaped brightly up.
Hatchets were flashing, wild forms leaping round,
And limbs quick tossing in death agonies.
I started, but a knee was on my breast,
A fierce red eye met mine, and gnashing teeth
Whence the hot breath came hissing, and as pealed
Shrill horrid whoops upon my shrinking ears,

I felt the hatchet sink within my side;
The sharp, cold knife swift glided round my brows,
My hair was clutched, and then with keenest pangs
The scalp was wrenched away; my sight grew black.
I woke to consciousness: my tortured head
Lay on a human breast; a human eye
Looked pitying on me. Soon the features broke
Upon my swimming memory; 't was the scout
Of the near village, whose kind hand was now
Sprinkling the stream's cool silver on my face,
While round me many an anxious neighbor stood.
"The morning sun had painted with its light
Palisades, roofs, and block-house, but the forms
Of the expected hunters darkened not
The sunbeam slanting in a narrow cleft
Through which the clearing-pathway pierced the woods;
The gaze was ceaseless from the picket-loops,
But still the hunters came not. Noon reeled red
Upon the summits of the distant pines,
And edged the threshold of the cleft with shade;
Still they were absent. Downward sloped the sun;
Blackened the cleft, and yet they came not thence.
At length a group, with fear-winged footsteps sought
The lost, and found them. Scalped in jellied gore,
The hunters lay, stone-dead. A movement slight
Told that I lived. The scout bound up my head
Stripped by the knife; and while these graves, round which

The fire-flies show and shut their gold-green lamps,
Were hollowed for my comrades, I was borne
To my low cabin by the block-house knoll,
Where with grim Death I fought a weary time,
But rose to vigorous strength and life at last."

THE BLOOD-STAINED.

An Indian-Summer noon. A purple haze,
Blurring hill outlines, glazing dusky nooks,
And making all things shimmer to the eye,
Is woven within the air. A woodland path
That leads me to a quiet glade, I tread.
The sunshine twinkles round me, and the wind
Touches my brow with delicate, downy kiss.
A stillness so intense around is breathed,
That the light crackling of the withered leaves
On which I tread sounds loudly. Dropped below,
The walnut clicks as though a pebble smote
On water, and the tiny beech-nuts, showered
By the gray-squirrel leaping from his branch,
Patter like rain-drops. Now the glade is reached.
Moss-mounds are scattered o'er it, and short grass
Clothes it with velvet. Through the midst, a stream
Laps, like a tongue, amid its pebble-stones,
And drips along its plants. Upon its bank,
Traced by the wood-cart, winds a narrow track
From the thick forest to the village near.
Upon the highest mound, a cabin rude,
Framed of rough, barky logs, and seamed with clay,
Once stood. A fragment of its roof is now

Slanted within the little area formed
By the decaying base. Within the square
The mullein lifts its pillar, and a web
Of blackberry brambles, spangled o'er in spring
With silver, and in autumn studded thick
With ebon gems, is twined. Here, years ago,
Lived an old hunter. Rough his deer-skin garb
And wild his features. Black and shaggy brows
Roofed the deep sockets, in whose gloomy depths
Glared fierce, keen eyes. Those couched and snake-
like balls
Ne'er met another's look, but with quick shift
Eluded, and if still the gaze sought his,
A frown drew up its coils upon his brow,
And from those cavernous depths malignant gleams
Shot sidelong as he turned. Deep mystery robed
The hunter. None his lonely cabin shared,
Save one gaunt hound, with grim and threatening look,
Whose savage growls, whene'er belated foot
Trod the night-shadowed glade, caused thrill of fear.
The chopper, wending homeward in the dark,
From his near wood-lot at the forest edge,
Heard horrid shrieks, and oaths, and frenzied shouts
In the old hunter's voice, from out the hut,
Ceasing as those deep warning growls arose
At the near-coming footstep. When abroad
Amid the haunts of men the hermit went,
He bore his rifle slanted on his arm,
With finger ever ready to the lock.
As through the village street he swiftly passed,

Shooting his subtle sidelong glances round,
It seemed as though his coming cast a shade
Upon the sunshine. Children ceased their play
And clung to one another till he passed.
And the old gossips, chattering in a group,
Paused and gazed after him with fearful looks.
His brain seemed struggling with insanity.
Once a strange sunset glared. The clouds were bathed
In a dark crimson; the same lurid hue
Gleamed to mid-heaven, and over earth the tinge
Seemed like spilled blood. The village groups in awe
Were gazing at the sight, when, suddenly,
The hunter, with the carcass of a deer
Slung o'er his shoulders, from the girdling woods
Came with slow laboring foot. The sunset streamed
Broadly upon him. As if turned to stone,
He stopped, — the carcass fell, and with strained eyes
And mouth agape he looked before, around,
Below, shuddered, — and then, with thrilling cry,
Sank on the earth. The foam stood on his lip,
Mingled with blood drawn by his gnashing teeth.
The villagers drew round and gazed with dread
Upon his writhing features. With a start
Then sprang he to his feet, and muttered, "Blood!
Blood! blood! all blood! the very sky and earth
Give witness of the deed. Ha! hide thy throat,
Spouting its red-hot gushes on my brow!
I do defy thee: ha! ha! ha! I stand
To battle with thee," drawing from its sheath
His keen, bright hunting-knife. "Away! away!

Or the lone camp-fire blow I strike again."
His eyes shone spots of fire; his long black hair
Seemed knotting with the agony impressed
On brow and cheek, but as the last dread words
Fell from his tongue, he started and looked round.
The maniac wildness vanished from his face,
And searching inquiry and deep alarm
Succeeded; subtle grew his serpent-eye,
And, lifting up the deer, he muttered low
Of sudden pains, and quickly left the spot.

Again — 't was such a glorious day as this;
The village children, I among the rest,
Went nutting in the woods. In merriest mood
We shook the hickory's ivory balls below,
And left a circle of green shells around
The mossy roots. Now mocking in our glee
The harsh, brief trumpet of the restless jay
Tossing among the thickets his plumed head
And fluttering his blue wings; now up the oak
Gazing, led thither by the shrieking yelps
Of the pet spaniel, shivering with delight
And dancing as on wires, until we saw
The squirrel's silvery fur within the leaves,
We toyed along, till came we to the edge
Of the dread glade. Upon the soft, sweet air
We heard a voice; now bubbling amid leaves,
Now choked, now lifted nearly to a scream.
It seemed as though the broken accents tried
To frame a prayer, but could not. Back we pressed —

Back from the sounds. But one bold, reckless boy
Trod with a cautious, oft-arrested step,
And face where curiosity o'er fear
Had triumphed, and upon the grassy glade
He saw the hunter prostrate; dashing now
His head upon the earth, and now with hands
Tight folded, stealing timid looks toward heaven,
But quickly dropping them, while those dread sounds
Came from his writhing form. He saw and fled.
One eve, — one winter eve, — upon the ice
Of a small lake, whose narrow foot wound in
Beside the glade, we glided fleet with skates
Until dark night. The rich Auroral fires,
Those lightnings of the frost, were kindled up;
Now skirting the horizon with bright tints,
Now shooting high, until a crimson arch
Bent across heaven. The reddened ice gleamed back
The radiance, and the snow in ghastly hues
Glared in the forests. While that splendid arch
Was brightest, from the glade mad screams outpealed
With groans and horrid laughter. Fear gave wings,
And to the sparkling hearth-fires of our homes
We hurried. Wild at midnight roared the storm.
The snow beat heavily on the window-panes,
And the sleet tinkled. From the neighboring woods
We heard the keen hiss of the yellow pine,
And the stern surging of the hemlock boughs
Fierce struggling with the blast. The wolf was out,
For now and then we heard his mournful howl
Blent with the forest-voices. Morning came,

With breathless atmosphere and brilliant sun.
The chopper, hastening to his hill-side lot
In his rude wood-sled, as his oxen slumped
Across the glade, saw, at the forest edge,
Wolves fiercely battling. Wrathful snarls he heard
And gnashing teeth; and quickly speeding back,
He led a hasty-summoned village group,
Each with his rifle, to the spot. A shower
Of deadly bullets piled the wolves around,
Or drove them to the forests. When the heap
Of shaggy limbs, thick spotted with fierce eyes,
Had ceased their writhings, toward them stole the group.
The fragments of a human form were strewed
In the wild midst; white bones were here and there
Scattered among long strips of gory flesh
And shreds of garments. Near them lay a hound,
Mangled and crushed into a shapeless heap.
A face, half peeled from brow to chin, was seen
Among the fragments. Gazing with deep awe,
The simple villagers those features knew;
And looking at each other, whispering low,
And calling up each scene that made the life
Of the rude hunter such dark mystery,
They broke a grave within the frozen earth,
Gathered, in shuddering silence, the remains,
And left the blood-stained to his last repose.

SUNSET ON SHAWANGUNK MOUNTAIN.

A PARADISE of beauty in the light
Poured by the sinking sun, the mountain glows
In this soft summer evening. Dark and cool
The shadow of the opposite hills is spread
O'er Mamakating, save where brightly stretch
The edges of the golden mantle, wove
In the rich loom of sunset, and thrown o'er
The earthen monarch's form. Within the light
Sparkles the stream, the shaven meadows glow,
The cornfields glitter, smiles the kindled grain,
Farm-house and barn cast far their ebon shapes,
While the long tip of the hay-barrack lies
Upon the clubbed foot of the midway pine
Bristling on Shawangunk. But within the midst
Of the sweet valley stand the village-roofs,
With the first shiftings of the twilight gray
Upon their outlines. Onward slowly creeps
The mighty shadow ; no more shines the stream,
Meadow and cornfield darken, and the grain
Looks faded ; deeper swim the twilight shades,
Until the hollow links in blended gloom.
On still the shadow steals ; the mountain's foot
Is blackened, but a glow of quivering tints

Yet plays upon its breast. Half light, half gloom,
Now shows the slope. Up, up the shadow creeps
Toward the steep brow; the lustrous gloss peels off
Before it, till along the ragged top
Smiles a rich stripe of gold, that up still slides
Until it dwindles to a thread, and then,
As breath glides from a mirror, melts away.

Now as I tread the twisting cattle-path
Along its base, the cool air on my brow,
I hear a ceaseless twitter running through
The trees and bushes from the nestling birds,
Blent with the long-heaved sighing of the pine,
The buzz of insects on their skimming wings,
And the deep-throated gurgle of the brook
Down in the black ravine. A mingled voice
The hollow too upsends: low human talk,
Shrill whistlings, tones of children at their play;
The cow-bell tinkling in the meadow-grass;
The loud, quick bellow echoing down the vale;
The bleat, the barn-yarn clarion, and the wheel
On the ear shaking; yea, so still the air,
I hear the pleasant rustling of the scythe
Cutting its keen way through the long, deep grass,
And even the fitful stamping of yon horse
Standing within a corner of the rails
Bounding his pasture.
Back I trace my path.
The twilight deepens. Shadowy, vast, and grim
The mountain looms, while on the western hills

The darkness gathers in one gloomy cloud;
O'erhead the stars out-tremble, and the moon,
Late cold and blind, is filling rich with light;
And as the east grows duskier, shadows faint
Are thrown upon the earth, till soft and sweet
The moonlight bathes all nature in its calm
And solemn joy. Oh holy, holy hour!
Hour of pure thought, when worldly cares depart, —
When heaven seems near the weary one of earth,
And God o'erbending with inviting smile.

ANGLING.

THE south wind is breathing most sweetly to-day,
The sunshine is veiled in a mantle of gray,
The Spring rains are past, and the streams leap along—
Not brimming nor shrunken—with sparkle and song;
'T is the month loved by anglers,—'t is beautiful June!—
Away then, away then, to bright Callikoon!

A narrow wild path through the forest is here,
With light, tiny hoof-prints,—the trail of the deer!
Beside and above us, what splendor of green!
The eye can scarce pierce the dense branches between.
How lightly this moss-hillock yields to the foot!
How gnarled is yon bough, and how twisted that root!
What white and pink clusters the laurel hangs out;
The air one deep hum from the bees all about!
The chestnut—'t is gala day with her—behold,
Her leaves nearly covered with plumage of gold!
While thick in the depths of the coverts below,
The blackberry blossoms are scattered like snow.
High up, the brown-thrasher is tuning its lay,
And the red-crested woodpecker hammers away;

The caw of the crow echoes hoarse from the tops;
The horn of the locust swells shrilly, and stops;
While knots of bright butterflies flutter around,
And seeks the striped squirrel his cave in the ground.

We break from the tree-groups: a glade deep with
grass;
The white clover's breath loads the sense as we pass;
A sparkle — a streak — a broad glitter is seen, —
The bright Callikoon through its thickets of green!
We rush to the banks: its sweet music we hear,
Its gush, dash, and gurgle all blent to the ear.
No shadows are drawn by the cloud-covered sun;
We plunge in the crystal, our sport is begun.
Our line where that ripple shoots onward, we throw;
It sweeps to the foam-spangled eddy below;
A tremor, a pull, the trout upward is thrown,
He swings to our basket, — the prize is our own.

We pass the still shallows; a plunge at our side, —
The dive of the muskrat, its terror to hide.
A clamor is heard, spots are darting from sight, —
The duck with her brood speeding on in affright.
A rush, — the quick water-snipe cleaving the air;
We pass the still shallows, — our prey is not there.

But here, where the trunk stretches half o'er the
brook,
And slumbers the pool in a leaf-shadowed nook,
Where eddies are dimpling and circling away,

Steal gently, for here lies the king of our prey.
Throw stilly: if greater the sound meets his ear
Than the burst of a bubble, you strike him with fear;
How cautious his touch of the death-hiding bait;
The rod now is trembling: wait! patiently wait!
A pull, — raise your line, yet most gently, — 't will bring
The credulous victim more sure to his spring;
A jerk, and the angle is bent to its length,
Play the line from the reel or 't will break with his strength!
He darts round in foam, but his vigor is past;
Draw steadily to you, — you 'll have him at last!
Raise up, but beware that strong struggle and gasp,
And the noble snared creature is filling your grasp.
How bright with the water-gloss glitters the pride
Of his brown-clouded back, red and gold spotted side!
But we leave the reft scene of the dead monarch's reign,
Like a despot that moves on to triumph again.

The voice of the rapid now burdens the air, —
Approach, for our prey's crowded city is there!
Here whirlpools, there eddies; here stillness, there foam;
We ply well our efforts, — no further we roam.
Our baskets we fill, but our muscles are tired,
And a shade in the sky tells that day has expired;
The robin has chanted his vespers and flown;
The frog from the creek has commenced his trombone;

The spider has ceased his slight furrow to show ;
The brown sprawling shrimp seeks the pebbles below;
The bank then we clamber, our home-path resume,
The torch-bearing fire-fly to lighten the gloom,
And dreams of our sleep-fettered pillow restore
Our day-sport, distorted but pleasing, once more.

DEER SHOOTING.

The east is now dappled with dawning of light,
To the woods for the deer ere the sun is in sight!
The white frost has spread its fresh, silver-like veil,
And if a hoof passes, it tells us the tale.
The hound in swift gambols darts hither and yon,
We shoulder our rifles, and rapidly on.

Each limb how elastic,—how bracing the air!
Hurrah, boys, what know we of sorrow or care!
Our veins tingle wild with delight, as we feel
The breath of the autumn morn over us steal;
The herds to their pastures are wending along,
And hark! the first robin has burst into song!
The hawk leaves the pine, in slow circles to sail,
And in the brown stubble-field whistles the quail;
Tread faster! for now the deer glides from the shade
To drink at the streamlet, and feed in the glade;
If longer we loiter, we 'll seek him in vain,
He 'll soon make his couch in the thickets again.

His haunts we approach: creep on cautious and slow,
The stir of a branch our dread presence will show;

His haunts we approach; scan the glade-grass, and look
For his prints in the soft oozy marge of the brook;
Here 's a dash of the moss from the rock; there has sunk
His hoof in the brown brittle dust of the trunk;
Lead the hound to yon thicket! these tracks all around
Proclaim that the run-way at last we have found.

His rich rainbow banner hath Autumn unrolled,
The woods blaze in splendors of crimson and gold;
The leaves cutting sharp on the soft sapphire sky
Shine clusters of jewels suspended on high;
The dream-like and delicate light melting through
Seems changed where it falls to an opal-like hue,
So vivid and varied the colors that glow
On the undergrowth spread, a deep mantle, below.
With canopy o'er, rich as monarch could claim,
And rifle on shoulder I wait for the game.
As breathings I hold, the hound's music to hear,
The trickle of waters comes meek to my ear;
His hollow-toned trill the dark cricket repeats;
Like watch-ticks, the spider's quick regular beats;
In contrast, the glee of the grasshopper-throng
With the catydid's solemn monotonous song;
Then wearied with listening, I smile as, in ire,
The milksnake out-launches his pronged tongue of fire,
And on the prone beech, the coxcombical crow

Struts lordly, as if his black plumage to show:
But hark to that sound stealing faint through the wood!
Heart hammers, breath thickens, swift rushes the blood!
It swells from the thicket more loud and more near,
'T is the hound giving tongue! he is driving the deer!
My rifle is levelled, swift tramplings are heard,
A rustle of leaves, then, with flight like a bird,
His antlers thrown back, and his body in motion
With quick rise and fall like a surge of the ocean,
His eyeballs wide rolling in frenzied affright,
Out bursts the magnificent creature to sight.
A low cry I utter; he stops, bends his head,
His nostrils distended, limbs quaking with dread;
My rifle cracks sharp, he springs wildly on high,
Then pitches down headlong, to quiver and die.

On the trail now comes, leaping and panting, the hound,
And I hear the shrill whoop of my comrade resound;
Up wheels the broad sun, his fresh joy giving light
The innermost depths, striking quick into sight:
A twitter and flutter awake in the trees;
The stream casts its white curling breath to the breeze;
As under our burden we stagger along
The sociable wren bids good-morrow in song,

But the chatterbox squirrel is swelling with wrath,
And stamping, lets drop his brown nuts in our path;
We heed not his antics, but trudge on amain,
And stand, spent with toil, at our threshold again.

FOWLING.

A MORN in September! the east is yet gray,
Come, Carlo! come, Jupe! we 'll try fowling to-day:
The fresh sky is bright as the bright face of one
A sweeter than whom the sky looks not upon;
And those wreathed clouds that melt to the breath of
the south
Are white as the pearls of her beautiful mouth;
My hunting-piece glitters, and quick is my task
In slinging around me my pouch and my flask;
Cease, dogs, your loud clamor! you 'll deafen my brain;
Keep your breath for the sport, and your gambols restrain.

Here, leave the geese, Carlo! to nibble their grass,
Though they do stretch their long necks and hiss as
we pass;
And that fierce little bantam, that flies your attack,
Then struts, flaps, and crows with such airs, at your
back;
And the turkey, too, smoothing his plumes in your
face,
Then ruffling so proudly, as leave you the place;
Ha! ha! that old hen bristling up mid her brood,
Has taught you a lesson, I trust, for your good, —

By the wink of your eye, and the droop of your crest,
I see your maraudings are now put at rest.

The rail-fence is leaped, and the wood-boughs are round,
A moss-couch is spread for my foot on the ground;
A shadow has dimmed the leaves' amethyst glow,
The first glance of Autumn his presence to show!
The beech-nut is ripening above in its sheath,
Which will burst with the black frost and drop it beneath;
The hickory hardens snow-white in its shell,
The butternut's globes show more large in the dell,
The chestnut is changing its hue in its burr,
The cones are full-grown on the pine-tree and fir,
The hopple's red berries are tinging with brown,
The tips of the sumach have darken'd their down,
The white brittle Indian-pipe lifts up its bowl,
The wild turnip's leaf curls out broad like a scroll,
The cohosh displays its white balls and red stems,
The braid of the mullein is yellow with gems,
While its rich spangled plumage the golden-rod shows,
And the thistle yields stars to each air-breath that blows.

A quick startling whirr now bursts loud on my ear, —
The partridge, the partridge, swift pinioned by fear;
Low onward he whizzes, Jupe yelps as he sees,
And we dash through the brushwood to note where he trees;
I see him, — his brown speckled breast is displayed

On the branch of you maple that edges the glade;
My fowling-piece rings, Jupe darts forward so fleet,
Ere I load he lays down the dead bird at my feet.
I pass by the scaur-berries' drops of deep red
In their green creeping leaves, where he daintily fed;
And his couch near the root, in the warm forest-mould,
Where he wallowed, till sounds his close danger fore-
told.
On his branch, the bright oriole dances and sings,
With rich crimson bosom and glossy black wings;
And the robin lights warbling, then flutters away,
For I harm not God's creatures so tiny as they;
But the quail, whose quick whistle has lured me along,
No more will recall his strayed mate with his song;
And the hawk, that is circling so proud in the blue,
Let him keep a lookout, or he 'll tumble down too:
He stoops, the gun echoes, he plunges beneath,
His yellow claws curled, and fierce eyes glazed in
death.
Lie there, cruel Arab! the mocking-bird now
Can rear her young brood without fear of thy blow;
And the brown wren can warble his sweet little lay,
Nor dread more thy talons to rend and to slay;
And with luck, an example I 'll make of that crow,
For my green sprouting wheat knew no hungrier foe;
But the black rascal seems from his summit to scoff,
And as I creep near him, he croaks, and is off.

The woods shrink away and wide spreads the morass,
With junipers clustered, and matted with grass,

Trees standing like ghosts, their heads splintered and
bare,
O'erhung with pale lichens, like age-whitened hair,
The tamarack here and there, rising between,
Its gray mossy boughs tufted over with green;
With clumps of dense laurels, and brown-headed flags,
And thick slimy basins black dotted with snags:
Tread softly, now, Carlo! the woodcock is here;
He rises, his long bill thrust out like a spear;
The gun ranges on him, his journey is sped,
Quick scamper my spaniels and bring in the dead:
We plunge in the swamp, the tough laurels are round, —
No matter, our shy prey not lightly is found;
Another up-darts, but unharmed in his flight, —
Confound it! the sunshine then dazzled my sight!
But the other, my shot overtake as he flies, —
Come, Carlo! come, Carlo! I wait for my prize;
Another, another, till, proofs of my sway,
From my pouch dangle heads in a ghastly array.

From this scene of exploits, now made birdless, I pass,
Pleasant Lake gleams before me, a mirror of glass;
My boat 's by the margin, with branches supplied,
From the keen-sighted duck my approaches to hide;
A flock spots the lake now, — crouch, Carlo, below, —
And I move, with light paddle, on cautious and slow.
By yon wide lily-island, its meshes that weaves,
Of balls rich and golden, and large oval leaves,
I watch them; how bright and superb is the sheen
Of their plumage, gold blended with purple and green;

How graceful their dipping, — how gliding their way, —
They are almost too brilliant to mark as a prey!
One flutters enchained in those brown speckled stems,
His yellow foot striking up bubbles like gems,
Another with stretched neck darts swiftly across
To the grass, whose green points dot the mirror-like gloss;
But my labor I cease, their wise leader the drake,
Eyes keen the queer thicket afloat on the lake;
They group close together — both barrels — oh dear,
What screaming and diving and splashing are here!
The smoke-curls melt off as the echoes rebound, —
Hurrah! five dead victims are floating around.

But "cloudland" is tinged now with sunset, and bright
On the water's smooth polish point long lines of light,
The headlands stretch likewise their dark shadows o'er,
And I pull with my spoil once again to the shore.

SPEARING.

The lake's gold and purple have vanished from sight,
The glimmer of twilight is merged into night,
The woods on the borders in blackness are massed,
The waters in motionless ebony glassed,
The stars that first spangle the pearl of the west
Are lost in the bright blazing crowds of the rest;
Light the torch! — launch the boat! — for to-night we
    are here,
The salmon, the quick-darting salmon, to spear.

We urge our light craft by the push of the oar
Through the serpent-like stems of the lilies near shore,
And turn the sharp prow at yon crescent-shaped cove,
Made black by the down-hanging boughs of its grove;
The meek eddy-gurgle that whirls at our dip,
Sounds low as the wine-bead which bursts on the lip;
On the lake, from the flame of our torch, we behold
A pyramid pictured in spangles of gold,
And the marble-like depths on each side of the blaze
Are full of dark sparkles, far in as we gaze;
The loon from his nook in the bank, sends a cry;
The night-hawk darts down, with a rush, through the
    sky;

In gutturals hoarse, on his green slimy log
To his shrill piping tribe, croaks the patriarch frog;
And bleat, low, and bark, from the banks, mingle faint
With the anchorite whippoorwill's mournful complaint.
We glide in the cove; let the torch be flared low!
The spot where our victim is lurking, 't will show;
Midst the twigs of this dead sunken tree-top he lies,
Poise, comrade, your spear! or farewell to our prize!
It darts; to the blow his best efforts are bent,
A white bubbling streak shows its rapid descent;
He grasps it as upward it shoots through the air,
Three cheers for our luck! — the barbed victim is there!
Give way, boys! give way, boys! our prow points to shore,
Give way, boys! give way, boys! our labor is o'er.
As the black mass of forest our torch-light receives,
It breaks into groups of trunks, branches, and leaves:
Low perched on the hemlock, we 've blinded with light
Yon gray-headed owl! — see him flutter from sight!
And the orator frog, as we glide with our glow,
Stops his speech with a groan, and dives splashing below;
One long and strong pull, the prow grates on the sand,
Three cheers for our luck, boys! as spring we to land.

"SEEK AND YE SHALL FIND."

A FAIR young girl, one golden summer day
Was wandering through a wood. The two whose love
Guided the tottering steps of infancy,
Had gone on high to wear bright wings and raise
Sweet anthems with the angels; she was left
The world's wild tempest to sustain alone.
Yet had her mind been filled with love for God,
Taught that He e'er was present, that His eye
Looked always on her, and His holy arm
Circled her in protection; and when Death
Was fastening heavenward pinions to the one
The last to leave her, as a mother's voice
Trembled upon her ear, she heard in awe,
Heard as her tears fell fast, that voice implore
The Father, Him who reigns in highest heaven,
To look upon the helpless child on earth,
And guide, and guard, and bless her. Since that hour
Oh! ever after, did her childish heart
Thrill and hush deep within itself, as thought
Wafted that death-bed scene, and in her ear
That broken voice was whispered. She had looked
In the soft twilight, hour of balm and dew,
In the deep night magnificent with stars,

In golden morn, and in the gorgeous set
Of the proud sun, and asked in prayer for God,
For God, her Father! and, oh blessed thought!
The Father of the loved ones passed away.
But naught, oh naught had met her eye or ear
To tell her of His presence. She was sad.
Her footsteps now were straying in the bright
And glorious summer noontide. Fresh and green
The leaves hung round her; overhead the sky
Seemed one bright smile; rich streaks of sunshine glanced
Like pointing fingers through the crowded stems,
And little birds, with soft-toned songs that seemed
Tuned for her ear, flew round her; tiny flowers
Wooing her touch were nestling in their nooks,
And all was peace and beauty. On a mound
Sloping like velvet, sank her girlish form.
Soft murmurs in the grass, a purling voice
In the near rill, a low, deep organ tone
Thrilling the pine-tree, lulled each sense, and sleep
Glided across her with its downy touch.
The ground-bird tripped beside and looked askance,
Then whirred away. The squirrel gazed and barked
And leaped into its bush. A straying fawn
Bleated in fear as his large staring eye
Met the prone form, and still she slumbered on.
A sweet, sweet dream enchained her: in her view
Two radiant shapes, around which sparkled still
The light that flashes from the "Great White Throne,"
Stood, every moment brightening, and soft sounds

Like far-off echoes, crept upon her ear.
The pure forms pointed round, the melting tones
Bade her eyes open and behold her God :
Just then a robin perched upon the pine
Pouring a gush of music, and she woke.
A mist seemed vanishing from her eye, — a veil
Seemed waving from her mind. She looked, — a light
Steady and clear, streamed broad within her heart,
And she saw God. Yes ! God was in the sky
Cloudless and bright above her; in the flower
That breathed beneath; in the rich fingered gold
Of the slant sunshine; in the emerald leaves
O'ercanopied : His voice was in the grass
Murmuring around, the stream, and organ pine ;
And bending low her knee and shedding tears
More sweet and soothing than she e'er had known,
She lifted up her childish voice and prayed.

FAITH.

If that high faith, whose holy beam
The future's midnight turns to day,
Be but delusion's feverish dream,
Returning reason sweeps away,
Oh who could nerve against despair,
When storms surround the staggering bark!
Oh who his weary burdens bear
Along a path so cold and dark!

The keen regret, the wasting grief,
The tears that make life's daily showers,
Oh where from these could come relief!
Oh where! if that dark creed be ours!
Better at once to end our pain,
In the hushed grave our sorrows cast,
Than drag along the galling chain,
And have no goal to reach at last.

But if that Faith that heavenward glows
Sheds on our hearts its radiance clear,
Then come, oh Earth! with all thy woes!
We care not for our trials here.

The soul, the soul can never die;
  Away all clouds will soon be driven;
Its goal is yonder glorious sky,
  Its everlasting home is heaven.

THE FORSAKEN ROAD.

In the deep bosom of the wilderness,
Arbored with green, now hidden by the leaves
Dropped at the breath of Autumn, seaming here
The hollow wet with oozing springs, and there
Traced lightly on the firm and level glade,
Winds, in two wheel-marks, a forsaken road.
Now it is lost within a sward of grass
Spread pleasantly, with scattered groups of trees, —
A place to lie in, when the summer sun
Throws broken gold; thence strikes it through the
shade,
With time-stained blazes on the thronging trunks
Hacked either hand. Within the densest spot,
A pine has stretched its giant barricade,
Bulging with knots and forked with splintered twigs,
The shroud-like moss o'ermantling; as it lies
So motionless, so powerless in decay,
I start to think its shattered summit once
Flaunted its daring challenge to the storm,
And told its fall in thunder. Still the wreck
Hath pleasant uses; its high twining roots
Are chambers for the squirrel, and its frame
Keeps bare a stripe of earth strewn o'er with mast

From the white drift that blocks the opposite side,
So that the tenants of the base might steal
In the brief glimpses of the winter sun
To find the scattered treasures.

Onward still
I trace the road; tall saplings in the midst,
Then tawny grain-cracked fragments crumbling fine
As my foot sinks within them; then a mound
Of the sweet, low-stemmed wintergreen; a bridge
Of logs then lying crosswise o'er a stream,
Gaping with chasms and tottering dank with age, —
A frail support; until the stone-piled wall
Cuts sharp across, and smiling farm-fields hide
All traces of the pathway.

As I tread
The lonely road, now scaring with my steps
The whizzing partridge, hushing with my form
The thrasher's song, and baring with my knife
The darkened hack o'erlaid with bark and rings
That years have circled, I give rein to thought,
And images throng round me. First the deer
Seeking the lick, leaves prints; the midnight wolf
Scenting his prey, tramps o'er; the red-man fierce,
Treads in the faint but noted marks, lest moss
And mould should show his trail. In after years
His compass the surveyor sets, and carves
Rude letters on the trees that, gifted thus
With language, tell the windings of the way.
And then the emigrant's huge wagon-tent
Gleams white between the trunks, with household goods

Piled in and dangling round; and midst them grouped
Childhood and matron age, the flock and herd
Straggling behind, the patriarch and his sons
Trampling before with axes, hewing wide
The underbrush, and bridging o'er the streams,
And kindling in the dell, when frowns the night,
Their bivouac-flame for slumber. Then with toil
The settler trudges o'er, his shoulders bent
Beneath his burden, from the distant mill,
To feed his famishing children. And as Time
Smooths the rough clearing to the smiling field,
The heavy wagon jolts across the roots
To the far market, and the tardy wheel
Therefrom bears loads of rustic merchandise.
And then as scattered walls of logs are merged
Into thick village roofs, the forest road
Is left, for the smooth spacious thoroughfare
Linking the hamlet to the river-side.

How like this lonely road, the track of life!
Wild passions rage along the path of youth
Till Reason's compass points the devious way.
Determination follows: hewing down
The barriers with the edge of energy,
Bridging o'er fortune's many adverse streams,
And lighting sorrow's frequent night with flame
Of solace till the morrow. Trials come:
Our hearts are strong with fortitude, and still
We tread beneath the burdens of our care,
For those we love are cherished. Then as home

Brightens to comfort, in our daily path
We reap reward of hardship ; and as joys
Cluster around us, the smooth, easy course
Of peaceful being leads us to the grave ;
And the rough early road is shunned, for Time
To shroud its varied surface from our thoughts ;
With proud Ambition lying prone across,
A dead and shattered wreck ; yet sheltering close,
(Its fragments turn'd by dire experience
To holier use than when it stood erect,)
By stern remembrance of its miseries,
Its wrestling warfare and its rending fall,
Home feelings, and the gentle ties of love,
From perishing in the snow-drifts of the world.

HOME.

Home of the soul! thy light appears
  A star to guide man's gloomy way,
When, pilgrim in this waste of years,
  His faltering step is turned astray;
Hope lends her pinions to his feet,
  Faith sheds its balm within his breast,
And tireless, on he speeds to greet —
  Prize of his toils — the goal of rest.

Darkly the night hath frowned on high,
  Roughly the path before hath spread,
And the fierce tempest, sweeping by,
  Hath beat upon the wanderer's head.
But through the night streams, pure and warm
  Upon the path, a pointing ray;
A hand is with him in the storm,
  To guide and guard, — his strength and stay.

Oh who would linger here, when Home
  Hath bliss that fancy never drew!
Oh why should footstep ever roam,
  When heaven shines o'er our mental view!

Home, glorious Home! earth's darkest sky
 And stormiest path we calmly brave,
For the bright wafting wings that lie
 In waiting for us at the grave.

MOONLIGHT.

FROM her blue sky-throned height
The moon looks down upon the silent scene,
Changing the gloom of night
To sparkling silver, with her magic sheen.

A solitary cloud
Steals o'er her orb, which paints a halo there ;
On floats the transient shroud,
Curls by that star-gem, and dissolves in air.

Yon lofty mountain-pile
Spreads a vast shadow on the glittering ground,
Its summit like an isle
Looming o'er billowy vapors wreathed around.

Within the templed wood
I wander lone ; sublimely still it stands
Enshrined to solitude, —
A green majestic fane — "not made with hands."

There frowns Night's blackest hue ;
And there a gleam is shot along the grass,

Seeming, to Fancy's view,
Spread for the fairies of the spot to pass.

Moonlight! it hath a spell
Like music sweet and low, — of feelings deep,
Of joys too bright to dwell,
And thoughts that come and sadden till we weep.

And blest, oh blest those tears!
The present's stern realities depart;
And other, happier years
Crowd, with their sweet old memories, to the heart.

The wakened, lifted soul
Draws nearer to that heaven we view afar;
More brightly shines the goal, —
A ray shoots downward from our native star.

The cedar's pillared shade
Streaks the wild path; and steeped in lustrous gloss,
Where spreads yon dewy glade,
Gleam on my eye the thickets, grass, and moss.

My grateful brow I bare
To the soft fragrant wind-kiss; in thy sight
The darkness of despair
Brightens to hope, O pure and holy Night!

These silvered leaves and flowers,
Yon rich broad sky, God's mighty banner spread, —

Mountain and forest-bowers, —
A sacred awe upon my spirit shed.

One prayer, as low I kneel,
That when Death's night succeeds Life's stormy day,
My sin-freed soul may feel
A heaven-sent calmness as it glides away.

THE OLD BRIDGE.

Through a lone landscape creeps a marshy stream;
Dead trees have fallen across, and withered twigs
Float on its stealing surface; where it shrinks
In narrowest line, the fragments of a bridge
Still stretch, though in decay. Its platform once
Of lopped pine saplings, two hewed trunks sustained.
But now the point of one foundation-log
Slants deep within the mire, and not a trace
Is witnessed of the causeway.
When the bridge
Lay in its perfect shape, foot, hoof, and wheel
Passed o'er its sturdy frame; the forest twined
Its leafy bowers around, and through its vault
The bright bank-brimming streamlet merrily danced.
But the keen axe has swept its way amid
The woodlands, leaving here and there a tree;
And summer suns have drunk the streamlet's fount,
Until the waters filter through a marsh
Where the bridge-remnants rest mid pools of slime,
Grass tufts like streaming hair, and sedges green
Pointing like daggers. But the ruin still
Shows life and beauty round it, and itself
Forms to the eye a picture. Timid Spring

Smiles with her violet eyes from mossy nooks,
And on its taper stem the lily hangs
Its snowy bell, rich tongued with downy gold.
The chirping snipe alights and balances
Its gray-white shape ; the woodcock darts in line
Upward at morn, but drops again at eve
To feed upon the ooze below the logs.
One mighty pine, amid the straggling trees,
Lifts its unchanging pyramid to heaven ;
And when the sun is slant upon the scene,
The moss that clothes the fragments of the bridge
Glows like green velvet ; the pine-top is bathed
In golden lustre, while the streaming light,
Touching the remnants, makes a broad, bright track
Between them, and the sunset portals spread
As though to let the eye look through to heaven.

An emblem art thou, rude and mouldered wreck !
Of Age decayed and tottering. Strong in youth
Man bears his burdens ; Life's green objects stand
In myriads round him, and his feelings glide
In pure unwasted brightness through his breast.
But Time's hand grasps his form ; it, shatter'd, sinks :
Keen disappointment strikes the objects down
Until they lie in wrecks ; his feelings shrink
Beneath the glare of fierce reality,
Until they creep amidst the slime and weeds
Of craft and selfishness ; with broken frame,
Age rests then in the mire of slow decay.
But he is not forsaken : Childhood smiles,

Brightening his weary hours with merry looks;
Affection hangs above his couch of pain, —
A human blossom; volatile Youth draws near,
Pleased with his presence; Ardor oft forsakes
His counsel, soars aloft, but comes again
To learn new wisdom, ere he wings afresh.
Mid the few scattered objects left to him,
One changeless hope looks upward to the sky.
And as Life's sun slants low, it touches him
With sanctity, illumes the towering hope
To more resplendent light, and makes the space
That separates from the portals of the grave
A golden pathway between him and heaven.

THE AMBUSH.

Old winding roads are frequent in the woods,
By the surveyor opened years ago,
When through the depths he led his trampling band
Startling the crouched deer from the underbrush,
With unknown shouts and axe-blows. Left again
To solitude, soon Nature touches in
Picturesque graces ; hiding, here, with moss
The wheel-track ; blocking up the vista, there,
In bushes ; darkening with her soft, cool tints
The notches on the trees and hatchet-cuts
Upon the stooping limbs ; across the trail
Twisting, in wreaths, the pine's enormous roots,
And twining, like a bower, the limbs above.
Now skirts she the faint path with fringes deep
Of thicket, where the checkered partridge hides
Its downy brood, and whence, with drooping wing,
It limps to lure away the hunter's foot
Approaching its low cradle ; now she coats
The hollow, stripped by the surveyor's band,
To pitch their tents at night, with pleasant grass,
So that the doe, its slim fawn by its side,
Among the fire-flies in the twilight feeds ;
And now she hurls some hemlock o'er the track,

Splitting its trunk that in the frost and rain
Asunder falls and melts into a line
Of umber dust.

It was a summer eve.
Through the dark leaves, the low descending sun
Glowed like a spot of splendor from the shade
Of Rembrandt's canvas. In the wildest part
Of the wild road, where streaks of ruby haze
Were quivering, suddenly appeared a form
From the thick woods. His brow was stern and fierce,
And his keen eye was like a burning coal.
He bore a rifle, and within his belt
Glittered a knife. He bent his head aside
And listened breathlessly. The sunset breeze
Rising and sinking fitfully like sighs
Drawn by the forest and the twittering birds,
Alone were heard. He stooped his ear to earth,
Then starting up, with one quick bound he scaled
The prostrate body of a pine that lay
Like a low wall along the ancient road
Plumed with dense blackberry vines and crouched below.
Once more the usual quiet settled down.
The thrashers which had hushed their flutes when steps
Woke the green solitude, again perched near
And answered one another; from his grot
Again the squirrel glided in quick search
For the brown butternut, and even the fox
Peered with his sloping snout and glittering eye
From his dark den. The snapping of a twig

Broke on the air at length, and, treading swift,
A hunter, with his rifle at his side,
Strode by the pine-trunk. As he passed a shot
Rang from the covert. Up the hunter leaped,
Then headlong fell, with quivering limbs and blood
Reddening the earth. The murderer from his lair
Sprang with a savage yell and pointed knife,
And bent above the dying. In his look
Glared fiend-like hate and gratified revenge.
He stamped his foot upon the form that writhed
Amid its gore, then spurned it with wild strength
Over and over, laughed in horrid joy
At every hollow groan, while broken words
Of some foul wrong hissed fiercely through his teeth
Until the wretched victim gasped and died.
Then, dragging through the brown and mouldering leaves
The lifeless shape, he cast it in a pit
Hollowed by Nature near the ancient road,
Filled it with branches, and with fearful smile
Left the wild scene to all its sweet repose.

NIGHT IN THE WILDERNESS.

THE sunset Angel lights the leaves,
  Here, casts his wing an upward glow,
And there, his slanting finger weaves
  Bright net-work on the moss below.
Amid the pine, now fading dim,
The wild-bird trills its vesper hymn,
  And from the arbored shade
Whose cool green gloom had roofed the heat,
The red-deer glides with timid feet
  To feed upon the glade.

Far down, the brindled porcupine
  Within his shelving cave has shrunk,
And, darting in an arrowy line
  The wild-bee seeks its hollow trunk.
Each songster couched within its nest,
Is softly twittering into rest;
  Silent the partridge-drum;
The frog-marsh echoes harsh and loud,
And from it the mosquito-cloud
  Streams with its constant hum.

Along the western mountain's brow
  The golden rim has passed away,
And a large star is glittering now
  Out from the sheet of pearly gray;
Below, the woods are wrapped in gloom;
The cedar lifts its sombre plume,
  The beech is one dark mass;
And blackness, thick and murky, lies
Where lately glowed the blended dies
  Of blossom, leaf, and grass.

But the wild forest is awake:
  The gray-owl sends his startling whoop,
And frequent long-drawn howls outbreak
  As swiftly scours the wolfish troop;
And now and then the panther's yell
Pierces the air with long keen swell
  So full of threatening doom,
The hunter by his watch-fire's gleam,
Starts, with his rifle, from his dream,
  And shudders at the gloom.

But now the leafy summits traced
  Against the spangled dome of sky,
With faint and glimmering threads are laced,
  And softer purple glows on high;
The east arch kindles pure and bright,
While a huge globe of blood-red light
  Through the tinged branches glares,
Till o'er the wood-tops climbs the moon,

And earth in all the pomp of June,
  Her dreamy splendor wears.

Diamonds are scattered o'er the ground,
  Arrows are glittering in the sprays,
And on yon rippling stream is wound
  A shifting web of sparkling blaze;
The trunks are streaked with pearly gleams,
And every leaf carved silver seems,
  Till column, roof, and wall
Of myriad sylvan temples, rear
Their graceful shapes distinct and clear
  Below this gorgeous pall.

The shouting owl has sought his den,
  Wolf-howl and panther-shriek are still;
Gayly the hunter leaves the glen
  For his lone cabin on the hill.
He notes with smiles the shy raccoon
Dipping his corn-ear where the moon
  Has bathed the stream with light,
And sometimes, as his footsteps crush
Dry leaf and twig, he hears a rush,
  And antlers dart from sight.

The moonlight fades, dawn struggles gray,
  Tree-tops in golden light are glossed,
A robin whistles, — soon his lay
  In myriad chorus-strains is lost:
The damp wind's breath of sassafras

Lifts to the boughs, — stoops to the grass, —
  All things are fair and gay;
Night with her sights and sounds is flown,
And with attendants of his own
  Bright smiles the Summer Day.

THE FIRST VIOLET.

Warm rains and fanning winds; the snow-drifts melt
Into swift rivulets, and the forest floor
Shows its leaf-carpet, while the roots again
Are seen, thick velveted with moss; above,
Branches are studded with their bursting buds,
Below, green plants are springing; from her sleep
Nature has wakened, and laughs out with joy.
The maple has not reddened, nor the beech
Plumed its slight sprays; but from the earth the fern
Thrusts its green, close-curled wheel, the downy sprout
Its two leaves, and the tassels of the birch
Are lengthening their brown links. From spot to spot
The merry carol of the bluebird sounds,
The gay-winged messenger the Spring sends out
To tell us of her coming.

Wandering on,

A tiny blossom nestling in the moss
Gladdens the eye, — the little violet,
Pencilled with purple on one snowy leaf,
And breathing its light fragrance on the air.
It starts at the first summoning of Spring,
And laying its slight delicate ear to earth,
Listens for her approaching tread, and then,

As the South tells her breath, and brown gaunt trees
Catch the first gleaming of her emerald robe,
It calls upon the wind-flower to arise,
And the stream-loving cowslip:
As the leaves
Then look from out their prisons, and the grass
Shoots from the hill-slopes, and the cherry shows
Its mass of snowy blossoms, the sweet thing
(Like modest merit in this thankless world)
Hides its meek head mid countless throngs of flowers.

Come to the forest, bright one! and I 'll show
How Nature can be like thy lovely self.
Pleasure and happiness and blessèd hope
Are now in all her teachings: I will cull
This little violet, emblem of thyself
In thy fresh spring of life, and all the grace
Of thy bright girlhood, when the future seems
A glorious Eden with no gloom to dim.
These snowy leaves are like thy stainless brow,
Which sorrow has not paled, nor care impressed;
These purple streaks within this fairy cup,
Pencilled so lightly and so delicate,
Are like the fringes of thy sweet dark eye;
And the soft perfume of this bee-sought shrine,
Like the rich breathing of thy ruby lips.
Yon pearly cloud amid the stainless blue,
Is like thy heart in its pure, holy sleep, —
No passion ruffling, writhing in no grief,
But fancying the world is like that sky.

So be it ever, bright one; may the sword
Of thy good angel guard thy paradise,
And life glide on, like music, to its close.

We will not wander far, for soon the cloud
Rent from stern Winter's mantle in his flight,
Will send its cold, bleak wind, and rain and sleet.
But when the sun grows warmer, and the grass
Is thick upon the glades, and myriad flowers
Make carpets for the fairies; when the winds
Are scented, and the glorious sunsets spread
Their crimson mantles, edged with burnished gold,
And when the night is molten with the moon,
And all is blessed peace, I 'll teach thee then
Nature's most high and holy mysteries.
She is a harp, whose strings are intertwined
Within our hearts, which when we touch them, yield
Sweet, solemn music, making pure our thoughts, —
Hushing wild passion's turbulence to peace, —
Soothing our sorrows, and restoring hope,
And guiding us, with gentle hand, to heaven.

JUNE.

THE loveliest of the seasons, radiant June,
Gladdens us with her presence; tardy Spring
Timidly glanced upon the sky and earth
That softened and grew green beneath her eye.
The hoarse blast ceased, and sweet the gentle South
Fanned the young blossoms, and the downy buds,
Those fairy cradles of the flowers and leaves:
And mid the melody of leaping streams
The birds made warbling music.
Then the skirts
Of Winter's vanishing robe swept o'er again:
The black car of the tempest rolled on high,
The bluebird ceased its music, and the bee,
Lured by the transient sunshine to dart forth
With its rich hum, shrank back into its cell.
But the unceasing change in Nature's breast
Was working, and the kindly elements
Were nursing the pent principle of life
To greater strength and power, until it burst
Upon the wakened earth in leaves and flowers.

Summer hath bounded on us: loveliest sights
And sweetest sounds are echoing, smiling round;

The chestnut shows, amid its dark green leaves,
Its golden strings; the basswood shines in white;
And the slow locust opens to the sun
Its pea-bloom shapes of blossoms.
Where the wood
Arches its emerald depths, the mocking-bird
Mingles its mimic tones; the robin hears
His warble echoed from the neighboring bush;
The wren, shrill chattering, pauses, as its notes
Are doubled, and the russet ground-bird lifts
Its tiny foot, and shoots its bead-like eye
Around to see who mocks its light quick chirp.
On the hot sunny hill-sides, bristling, hangs
In branching drops, the dimpled strawberry
Through the short, weedy grass. The meadow shows
Its robe of purple clover, spangled o'er
With golden buttercups and daisy-stars
And dandelion-globes of silver down.

Beside yon pool that sleeps beneath a roof
Of blended branches, gemmed with ivy-urns
And laurel-chalices, the angler plies
His patient sport, and where the stream expands,
Fringed with thick alders, through the pasture-field,
In the cool crystal stands the toil-worn ox,
While the prone sheep upon the highest ledge
Pant wearily beneath the scorching sun.

A gray haze mantles round the mountain's brow,
And leaden streaks athwart the inky cloud

Proclaim the shower afar: the sky grows dim
And threadlike sprinkles glimmer in the air
With murmurings like a shell's. The haze moves on,
And soon the dense dark rain-sheets deluge earth,
Sounding most pleasant music. Branches dance,
Grass quivers, blossoms bow, while streams cast up
White leaping bubbles as the large drops beat
Upon their shaking bosoms: then a gleam
Of sunshine like a golden arrow shoots
Across the clouds that in huge fragments part,
Leaving white edges widening till they show
Glimpses of azure: silvery floating veils
Melt, and the naked sky is smiling o'er;
And as the black mass piles the frowning East,
The rainbow springs with all its glorious hues,
Its broad bright bases staining seemingly
Mountain or tree or cloud they rest upon;
The landscape in the slant rays of the sun
Sparkles with its innumerable gems,
As though a flood of silver had been poured
Molten upon it.
Now the West is made
One mighty opal by the sunset's pomp;
Tint follows tint, until the last bright ray
Fades from the mountain, and a softened light
Proclaims that Day has fled and Eve has come.

OBSERVATION.

Nature is full to overflow of charms,
For those that seek her with a searching mind
And the heart-portals open. Rude and lone
May seem the spot, but the instructed eye
And ear ne'er fail to find what wakens thought
And stirs emotion.
Let us thread our way
Through these close streets. A glance of sunshine paints
A golden track athwart this naked field
And up that knoll of pines. We tread along,
Up-clamber and descend. We find a chasm
Such as a torrent makes — a basin scooped
Like a dried pool within, and here we pause.
An elm is slanting o'er, its wreathing roots
Scarce holding to the banks; beneath the bulge
Of its broad base, a little mined-out nook.
Pebbles and sharp-edged stones are scattered round;
A pine above has shed its dry dead mass
Of fibres; here and there a cone is dropped
With horny wide-spread edges. Single plumes
Of the familiar brake, and blades of grass
Have struggled from the earth. Within the nook

Gleams a small coat of moss, and midway up
Upon a shelf of rock, a lichen-tuft.
There is no trace of beauty in the spot,
Naught, it would seem, to draw a glance or rouse
A feeling; yea, the foot might pass it by
E'en in close search of objects, unobserved.
But let us rest awhile upon this bank.
Listen! a murmuring sound arises up;
'T is the commune of Nature — the low talk
She holds perpetually with herself.
Let the ear separate the blended tones,
An orchestra of sounds! within the nook
A trill with pauses; on the rocky shelf
A light swift tick-tick; in the brake and grass
A merry strain; and, mingling all, a hum
As if the pine were breathing.
Now cast round
A scanning eye. This withered pine-tuft hold
Between you and the streak of mellow light
That like a slanting shaft of quivering motes
Glances yon opening through; five bars of gold
Joined at the base. Yon dark unsightly cone
Lift to the sun: what a rich hue of brown,
How sharp and delicate each oval edge!
Pick up that withered elm-leaf from the nook
Cast there by Autumn's blast: how beautiful
Those branching arteries! what myriad veins!
Yea, the whole leaf seems but a woven web
Of arteries and veins. Pluck yon tall brake:
A fairy chisel has been here at work,

Tracing exquisite beauty; waving lines,
Scallopings, dottings! perfect, wonderful!
Tear from that coat of moss a single branch;
A mimic pine-tree bristling o'er with fringe.
Sweep from the shelf the lichen; see this stem!
A pillar of pale green with crimson balls
Thick on its summit. Mark! the very stones
Seem sown with glittering gems: the pebbles smooth
And polished, have their light gray tint o'erstreaked
And shaded with rich varying hues.
O Thou,
Parent of Nature! awful Deity!
The earth is but a dot among the throngs
Of thy creation, yet in love hast Thou
Set round the swarming insects of this earth,
The signs that tell of Thee. The most minute
Are eloquent as the greatest. Thou hast given
An ear to hear, an eye to see, a mind
To understand; and yet the plainest things,
Those that are showered around us, we pass by
Unheeding; ear and eye and mind made dull
By objects mean and worldly. Oh that we
Would see the loveliness of Nature, hear
Her solemn harmony, and comprehend
The meanings that she utters. Constantly
Proclaim those meanings deepest wisdom forth;
Wisdom, that but applied to daily life,
Would make the beings that now grope their way
In gloom along a tangled narrow path,
Wiser and happier.

And oh! most of all
Those meanings point to Thee, eternal God,
Thee the Omniscient — the Omnipotent,
The Fount and Ocean of all earthly things.

THE LANGUAGE OF FLOWERS.

I DARE not whisper what I feel for thee,
But I will let the flowers, upon whose leaves
Hath Love its language written, plead my suit;
Then listen, lovely lady. First, I send
The rose of hundred leaves, ambassador.
The amaryllis next—an emblem, bright
And beauteous, of thyself; interpreter
Of my own thoughts, the cedar; then for thee
The pure white lily, for myself the pink
Red as the sky at sunset; mignonette
For thee, for me the bay-leaf; the green fern
For thee, the oak-geranium for myself;
The harebell next, another emblem sweet
Of thee, the currant for myself; again
The Austrian rose that breathes of thee such truth,
The jonquil whispering timidly for me.
The silver daisy and the jasmine wreathed,
Emblems again of thee; and for myself,
When the swift hours are warning me to leave,
I send the thyme to whisper thee the cause;
The orange-blossom next, more truth of thee,
With the rich musk-rose to complete the wreath.
Then, oh then, clustered with my hopes and fears,

Warm from repeated pressures to my heart,
And trembling with its beatings, close entwined
I give the myrtle's green and polished leaves
With the rose-hued chrysanthemum. With pride
I place thy wreath upon thy radiant brow,
And mine, with the red tulip in its midst,
I lay in deepest reverence at thy feet.

MUSINGS.

Once only have I met thee; once have heard
The soft and gentle music of thy voice
And gazed upon thy beauty; yet my heart
Is brightened with thy image, as the sky
Is kindled by the moonlight. Memory oft
Calls from the past that hour of magic spell,
And I am wrapped in day-dreams; on my ear
The warble of thy laugh falls clear and sweet,
Charming away the sorrow of my thoughts;
Thy form then glides before me with the grace
That fancy gives to angels, and I seem
Again within thy presence, and am blest.

I know it is in vain. I know thou art
To me as yon fair moon that dwells in heaven.
Yet often in my solitary walks
I take thee from my heart where thou art hid,
An idol in its shrine, and hold thee up
Before my mental vision. Brightness streams
Around me, and my soul is wrapped in bliss.
Fair forms throng round me, but I heed them not,
For thou art absent. Sweet looks glance around,
But thy soft, soul-lit, spiritual eye

Beams not among them, and thy fairy feet,
Moving in billowy lightness, pass not there.

Often when night is clustered with her stars,
Calling to thought, till, tired and sick at heart,
My head has sought its pillow, in sweet dreams
Thou comest to me. Then, entranced, I hear
Thy low rich tones of bee-like melody.
Thou seemest a pure spirit fresh from heaven,
With all its glory round thee, and I bend
In adoration blent with breathless awe.

The love I bore to Nature, and which glowed
Within me like a passion, has grown cold,
For every thought is thine. I feel not now
The deep delight I once felt, as I see
The sunshine showering gold upon the leaves,
The shadows dancing on the pleasant grass,
The purple mistiness of mountain-tops,
And the green gloom of valleys. Far away,
My pilgrim-heart is wandering to its shrine,
Laden with incense-offerings unto thee.

THE CAPTIVE.

The tempest of midnight shrieked loud through the sky,
Where the black shapes of clouds hurried torrent-like by;
And the moon struggled on through those surges of air,
Now seen, and now lost, in the hurricane there.

But forms in the forest trod silent and fast,
The darkness they sought, and wished louder the blast,
For the foe was before, and though shrouded in night,
Still keen ears and eyes watched each sound and each sight.

The hand grasped the hatchet — the belt bore the knife,
The tribe's sternest warriors were armed for the strife,
For their chief on his war-path had passed from the lake,
And, entrapped in the ambush, was kept for the stake.

And proud was that chief, though the fagots were piled,
And fierce eyes were gleaming, and curses were wild,

Though the knife gashed still wider wounds bleeding
and fresh,
And the red brand of torture hissed hot in his flesh.

Did he think of his lodge in the valley that stood?
Of the lake whose blue eye shone through fringes of
wood?
Of his bride who was weeping with terror and woe?
No ! he thought but of taunting and mocking his foe.

"How oft have ye trembled and crouched like the
deer,
At the sweep of my hatchet and dart of my spear!
Give me back but that spear and that hatchet, again
Will the blood of your bravest be sprinkled like rain.

"The scalp of thy father has dried in my smoke,
I seized thy young brother, his death-doom I spoke,
And my war-whoop was loud on the trail, when you
fled,
And the earth of your village was strewed with your
dead."

Their yells drowned his song, and the torch was
applied,
And a faint curl of flame caught the pile at his side,
But louder the strain waxed, and fiercer the eye,
As he called on their young men to teach them to
die.

But hark! from the forest's tempestuous gloom,
Shrill pealing from out the short hush of its boom,
Like shrieks of starved eagles, burst war-whoops, and fast
Whizzed thick clouds of arrows like hail on the blast.

With a leap like the panther's, the chieftain has sprung,
From his limbs are the bonds in the red fagots flung,
His blood-dripping hatchet a pathway has hewed,
And around him like leaves are his enemies strewed.

In its purple and gold, rose the morn in the east,
And lighted the vulture and wolf to the feast,
And shone on that lake where in victory's pride,
The chief hailed his village, his tribe, and his bride.

THE ALBANY RURAL CEMETERY.

When life's last breath has faintly ebbed away,
And naught is left but cold unconscious clay,
Still doth Affection bend in anguish deep,
O'er the pale brow, to fondly gaze and weep.
What though the soul hath soared in chainless flight;
Round the spurned frame still plays a sacred light,
A hallowed radiance never to depart,
Poured from its solemn source, the stricken heart.
Not to the air should then be given the dead,
Not to the flame, nor yet cold ocean's bed,
But to the earth, — the earth from whence it rose,
There should the frame be left to its repose.
There our great mother guards her holy trust,
Spreads her green mantle o'er the sleeping dust;
There glows the sunshine — there the branches wave,
And birds yield song, flowers fragrance round the grave.
There oft to hold communion do we stray,
There droops our mourning memory when away,
And e'en when years have passed, our homeward feet
Seek first with eager haste that spot to greet;
And the fond hope lives ever in our breast

When death, too, claims us, there our dust shall rest.
All these fair grounds with lavish beauties spread,
Nature's sweet charms — we yield them to the dead;
Those swelling uplands whence the raptured sight
Drinks in the landscape smiling rich and bright,
Woodlands and meadows, trees and roofs and rills,
The glittering river and the fronting hills;
That nestling dell with bowery limbs o'erhead,
And this its brother opening to the tread,
Each with its naïad tripping low along,
Striving to hide but freely offering song;
These old deep woods where Nature wild and rude
Has built a throne for musing solitude,
Where sunshine scarce finds way to shrub and moss,
And lies the fractured trunk the earth across;
These winding paths that lead the wandering feet
Through minster aisles and arbors dim and sweet;
To soothe thy discord into harmony,
O solemn, solemn Death, we dedicate to thee.

Here will his steps the mourning husband bend
With sympathizing Nature for his friend;
In the low murmur of the pine he 'll hear
The voice that once was music to his ear;
In the light waving of the bough will view
The form that sunshine once around him threw.
As the lone mother threads each leafy bower,
Her infant's looks will smile from every flower,
Its laugh will echo in the warbling glee
Of every bird that flits from tree to tree;

In the dead trunk laid prostrate by the storm,
The child will see its perished parent's form,
And in the sighing of the evening breath
Will hear those faltering tones late hushed in death.

Through these branched paths will Contemplation wind,
And stamp wise Nature's teachings on his mind;
As the white grave-stones glimmer to his eye,
A solemn voice will thrill him, "*Thou* must die;"
When Autumn's tints are glittering in the air,
That voice will whisper to his soul, "Prepare;"
When Winter's snows are spread o'er knoll and dell,
"Oh this is death," that solemn voice will swell;
But when with Spring, streams leap and blossoms wave,
"Hope, Christian, hope," 't will say, "there 's life beyond the grave."

THE REVENGE.

THE sunset poured among the crowded woods
In golden beauty, drenching them with light.
Long gleams of lustre lay upon the grass
Of a small valley-opening dropped with trees.
A streak of water bickered amid shrubs
Across the hollow, noiseless as a pulse,
And crept beneath a spreading alder-bush.
A holy silence brooded o'er the spot,
Save the scarce audible hum the forest yields
Even in deepest quiet. But the leaves
That spread their tawny carpet o'er the earth
Crackled; two forms glanced past the trunks whose throngs
Pillared the depths, and stepped within the dell.
Beside the rill they kneeled and drank, then threw
Their lengths upon the sward. The dark red skin,
High cheeks, and ebon eyes of one proclaimed
His Indian blood; the other, bronzed and wild,
Yet showed the white man's lineage. Both were garbed
Like hunters, with the rifle, pouch, and knife.
They talked with rapid gestures, merry laughs
Frequent from each, with now and then a swell

Of joyous song. At length their tones waxed loud,
The song and laughter ceased, their brows grew dark,
Abrupt and fierce their gestures, and their eyes
Devoured each other. Quick as thought, at length,
The white man darted on the Indian's breast
A giant blow. The savage started up,
His rifle lay upon the grass, but keen
Flashed in his grasp his knife; the wounded wolf
Springs not more fiercely at its foe, than he
On the white hunter; but the latter stood
With his long rifle aimed. One moment glared
The Indian at his comrade, then his face
Broke into one bright smile; he sheathed his knife,
Pressed his dark hand an instant on his heart,
And then extended it with dignity
Towards his companion, who, with honest warmth
Grasped it with words of pardon. Lifting then
Their rifles to their shoulders, through the cleft
In the encircling boughs, where went their path
They left the sylvan spot. The twilight soft
Trembled within the myriad forest-vaults
Although the hemlock-spires and maple-domes
Were burnished with rich glow. That passed away,
And all looked cold. The outlines of the trunks
Were shaded out, until long streaks of black
On lighter gloom alone told where they stood.
At length they reached a cabin, scarce discerned
Amidst a thicket. The long August drought
Had dried the saplings clustered round, and seared
The dense vines mantled o'er it, as though flame

Had scorched them. From its leathern hinges fallen
The door lay buried in the grass and fern
Of the luxuriant forest. Night was now
Fast closing, and the wearied hunters passed
Within the cabin. Half the barken roof
Away had rotted, and the autumn wind
Had sown a seed that now a sapling stood
Where once the hearth-fire glowed. Beside the stem
Upon a mound of moss, the hunters stretched
Their limbs for slumber. Onward rolled the hours,
And midnight came. The long-risen spotted moon
Poured its delicious light upon the woods,
Piercing with silver glance the aisles and vaults
Of the magnificent temple reared by God
For Solitude to yield Him ceaselessly
Incense from leaves and flowers, and upward roll
Grand crashing anthems of the mighty winds.
One ray streamed broad within the ruined hut,
And rested on the hunters. The smooth trunk
Of the young tree within the lustrous light
Shone like a shaft of pearl. The ray displayed
The Indian stealing from his comrade's side,
With motion like the gliding of a snake.
Undoing then his belt, he crept again
Close to the prostrate form, and with quick strength
Tight lashed him to the sapling. From his sleep
Startled so suddenly, the hunter gazed
Wildly around, then strove to break away;
In vain, his pinioned arms and breast were bound
As though in iron fetters to the tree.

He shouted to the Indian, but the click
Of flint on steel alone was heard without.
Just then a crimson streak shot brightly up
Athwart the door-space, as the lightning darts
Along the cloud; a crackling filled his ears,
And a shrill whoop pealed horrid on the air.
Again he strove to burst his bonds, the blood
Froze in his veins, his hair crept, and his heart
Swooned sick within him. Once more shouted he —
Again the whoop. The door-space was one glow;
The crevices were red, and tongues of flame
Shot through the smoke that poured within the hut.
"My God, the blow! the blow!" the sapling shook
With his convulsive strength in efforts vain.
The Indian stood without, a fiendish smile
Writhing his lip, fierce triumph on his brow.
Luridly leaped the avenging flames to heaven;
Night veiled her soft pure eye; the silvery blue
Was blotted out. Deep roared the raging fire,
And blending with it, piercing shriek on shriek
Pealed from the burning hut. The sapling flashed
In flame, and now and then quick tremblings shook
Its shape, as if wild strength were there at work.
At each shrill shriek, each tremor of the tree,
The Indian whooped, more glaring waxed his eye,
And his grim smile more fiendlike; but at length
Tottered the walls and sank; more fiercely sprang
The greedy element; it seemed as though
The fragments of the hut were swallowed up
In the quick crackling leap on high, so soon

They melted in the furnace roaring there.
No longer pealed the screams, and with quick hand
The Indian grasped some ashes at his feet,
Brushed them across his breast, and with a look
Of triumph left the spot of his revenge.

INDIAN SUMMER.

How quietly the year,
Beneath this soft-eyed season's gentle sway,
Falls in its full maturity away
On winter's frozen bier!
Like sunset gathering to its twilight close,
Or old age sinking to its last repose.

When first broke morning's light,
Volumes of fog a feathery ocean rolled,
The woods loomed glimmering from the misty fold,
Dimly the mountain's height
Seemed struggling in the thick and mantling screen,
And the bird sang and streamlet played unseen.

The mist has cleared away;
O'erhead the mild sun glows, a reddened ball,
And on the earth his placid glances fall,
While tranquil, meek, and gray,
The sky spreads, shaded with its fleece of cloud,
And azure glimpses breaking from the shroud.

The hill slopes soft and calm,
The fields still basking in the noontide light,

All seem my wandering footsteps to invite;
And with the south-wind's balm
Fanning in pure fresh kisses on my brow,
My paths is mid their haunts of quiet now.

Across the meadow sear,
And up the mount-side where the sumachs spread
Their downy branches tipped with clusters red,
And what a sight is here!
Arched but by sky and smiling in the ray
Of the warm quiet Indian Summer day!

The wood-spots dark and deep,
The upland vista, and the leaning hill,
The lake below, pure polished as a rill,
The sky in peaceful sleep,
The far-off mountains, like piled smoke-wreaths bright,
And valleys melting in rich purple light.

Late glowed a different scene;
When the chill air had sent its frosty showers,
The forests, burst to myriad gorgeous flowers,
Changed from their summer green,
The blue morn showed; while far and wide a blaze
Of differing splendor met the wondering gaze.

Within the sunny air
The foliage glittered to the wind's soft sigh,
Shone the lake's bosom like a sunset sky,
Beneath the glories there;

And where the mountains fired the heavens, it seemed
As though gigantic piles of jewels beamed.

And in the rainbow woods,
Here, was a fairy canopy unrolled
Of sumptuous crimson blent with brilliant gold,
There, the gemmed solitudes
Formed purple arches, bowers of every dye,
With opals showered on opals to the sky.

The storm then gathered o'er
With its chill rain, and with its rushing blast,
Upon the gusts their robes the mountains cast,
The wild lake sent its roar,
The pine hissed fiercely, and the forests woke
Their thunderings as the wind-surge on them broke.

But like an infant's rest,
Field, valley, hill, and wood, seem dreaming now
In a light glimmering film of purple glow,
And on the lake's smooth breast
The mist-wreaths sleep, or slowly curl across
As the breeze sportive darkens o'er its gloss.

With murmurs like a flute,
The streamlet glitters through the alder-sprays
In meteor sparkles or in broken rays,
Then on its ripples shoot,
In braided gushes, bending the long grass
And green fern-fringes bathed within their glass.

Along the forest way
I tread; the soft wind from the pine creeps down
And rustles in the beechen thicket brown,
Then whirls in eddying play
The withered leaves strown idly, rattling fast,
As showering falls the ripened sylvan mast.

The deer glides shadowy by;
The rabbit springs before me winged with dread,
The squirrel leaves the strewed nuts where it fed
With a low chirping cry,
And the quick flicker like a checkered speck,
Climbs the mossed oak and taps with darting neck.

The air, how calm and still!
Each gentle sound comes sweetly to my ear;
The falling nut, the bee-wing's music near,
The purling of the rill,
The chirp of bird, the sighing of the breeze,
And the far axe-blow echoing through the trees.

With what a feeling deep
Does Nature speak to us! Oh, how divine
The flame that glows on her eternal shrine!
What knowledge can we reap
From her great pages if we read aright!
Through her God shows His wisdom and His might.

The visions of our youth!
Bright as the autumn foliage are they found,

Robed in their glittering rainbows, all around,
Radiant in seeming truth,
Luring us onward, with their treacherous glow,
And brightening lovelier swifter as they go.

Then comes the threatening cloud;
Despair seems blackening in our adverse sky,
Frail as the leaves our brilliant visions die,
And where once brightly glowed
Fancy's enchanted Eden, naught appears
But a wide waste of sorrow and of tears.

But when our youth is past,
With its vain visions and its storms, serene
As yon mild sky, and peaceful as this scene,
Contentment smiles at last
Upon our way, and glorious hopes are given
To light our path, whose native home is heaven.

THE SEAT IN THE ROCK.

A RUDE, wild place. The long and narrow ridge
Ends in a rugged precipice of rock;
A slope between it and a shallow pond
Bristling with withered hemlocks and with stumps
O'erspotted. A faint narrow road winds by,
Here to the village — there, amidst the woods
Bordered by laurel-thickets, to a glade.
A jutting of the rock has formed a nook
Along its base. A cedar's giant trunk,
Dead, barkless, and stained black in spots by fire,
From the high bank above has pitched, and lies
With base upon the summit of the rock,
And fractured head upon the bank below,
A slanting ladder; and within a cleft
O'er a huge bulge upon the rugged wall,
Are birchen bushes, like green hanging plumes
In a gigantic helmet. At one spot
Within the nook, the back is hollowed out,
Shaping a seat. Naught is there to declare
Whether by freak of Nature or by man,
This shelf was scooped. Upon the fissured sides,
And the smooth slate that, laid in scales, compose
This little terrace, names and letters rude

Are graven. With the massive roof above
Spotted by lichen-scales, and looking out
On the grim pond, with its deep background woods,
Here have I sat in summer afternoons,
Watching the long, slim shadows of the trees
Slow creeping towards me, the rich haloed sun
Melting the outlines of the forest-tops,
Where it impended. In the hours of Spring,
When the damp softened atmosphere proclaimed
The coming rain to beat the frost from out
The torpid earth, so that its lap might smile
Again with flowers, here likewise have I sat
And listened to the voices of the pond,
Those surest prophecies of warmer hours,
Ringing like myriad tiny silver bells
Cheerfully on the ear.
Bright day-dreams oft
Have hovered o'er me in this lonely place,
And though its homely features might attract
Few to bestow a thought, yet Memory twines
Her fibres round it. Ruthless Time hath driven
The fairy dreams away, but still the spot
Is hallowed where they brightened.
Strange, most strange,
The power of Memory! with her kindling touch,
From the dim paintings of the past she brings
The golden tints in added brilliancy,
But leaves the shadows to their dusky rest,
Strange, strange her power! the porch of home, though
rude,

Is twined with fadeless roses; all its scenes
Are full of echoes wakened by her spell.
The trees have voices and the streams have songs,
And even the air seems gifted with a sound
Like a low wind with pleasure in its moan.
No tone that ever struck upon her ear
Is lost: no scene that ever met her eye
Can fade. The discords of this jarring world
May hush the tone, its change o'erlay the scene,
But still within her essence and upon,
It vibrates and is graven, and at last,
In some great self-convulsion, or in hours
We dream not of, will echo in the mind,
And stand revealed before its opened eye.

MONGAUP FALLS.[1]

THE heat spreads a pale shining glaze o'er the sky,
Like piles of carved brass, the clouds motionless lie;
The west hath not sent yet its soft kissing breeze
To stir the close air, or wake life in the trees;
With dull, weighty languor the frame is oppressed,
The shades dropped around bring no coolness or rest;
As we pant under shelter or melt in the glow
Our minds wander off to the regions of snow;
The cold, polished ice spreads its plain to our feet,
We skim in the keen wind rejoicing and fleet.
Then other sweet visions glide, changing the scene,—
The dim, vaulted forests, with twilights of green;
The stream dancing onward delicious and cool,
Here foaming a torrent, there coiling a pool;
The cavern with fresh dripping moss spotted o'er,
And water-drops tinkling like bells on the floor;
Hurrah, a thought strikes us! shake languor away!
The Falls of Mongaup will we visit to-day!

The rough springless wagon — two steeds under rein,
The harness eked out of rope, leather, and chain —

[1] These falls are in a wild and romantic stream called the Mongaup, in Sullivan County, State of New York.

Creak up to the inn-porch; — we wheel from the spot,
One horse in a canter, and one on a trot;
Along the broad turnpike we clatter and shake,
Like a hail-storm, with clouds of thick dust in our wake;
We clamber the hill, round the corner we tear,
Two wheels slanted downward, and two in the air.
Still plies the whip fiercely, our balance we find,
We dash down the slope with the speed of the wind;
The fences of serpentlike pine-roots we pass,
Scathed stump-spotted clearings and patches of grass,
With low crouching cabins of logs chinked with clay,
Long well-sweep, and wood-pile, and brown stack of hay.
The dark welcome forests spread round and on high;
The road winds in shadow with glimpses of sky;
Our steeds strike their hoofs on roots pared to a coil,
Our hubs graze the trees, from the banks plough the soil;
Like opposite cannon, logs point from the shade
Where once the prone pine its huge rampart had laid;
A branch now inclines its green archway so low
We stoop to avoid in our faces the blow;
We struggle through hollows, roll smooth over moss,
And jolt over logs the swamp-streamlet across,
Where we scare up the woodcock, quick catching a look
Of the rich-tinted sheldrake swift seeking his nook;
Then upward we labor; the steep ridge we crown,

Either side on the tops of tall trees looking down,
Our course alone pointed by time-blackened hacks
The pioneer-settler has marked with his axe.

That rustle! joy, joy! 't is the breeze moist and sweet,
Oh how the leaves dance its glad presence to greet!
It glides with smooth balm o'er our heat-beaded skin,
Each pulse feels its soothing — each breath draws it in,
It stirs the wet hair from our brows with its kiss,
And we yield in delight to the delicate bliss;
The aspens shake loosely like fountains in play,
The maples quick change their green colors to gray,
The hemlocks give murmurs like millions of bees,
There is patter like rain in the slight birchen trees;
Wherever those pinions are fanning their flight
There coolness and music — there life and delight.

We leave the wood-shadows, dark, breezy, and sweet;
Again, like a burning-glass, beats down the heat;
The low-gabled school-house we pass on our way,
The white-headed urchins shrill shouting in play;
The road down the hill by a torrent seems rent,
Loose stones and deep gullies — a break-neck descent —
We glide o'er the flat, round the angle we spin,
And halt, with a shout, at the Forestburgh Inn.
In a room lined with benches, and sprinkled with sand,
At a picketed nook, the boys clamorous stand,
Where bottles and glasses and rolls of cigars
Show tempting behind the half-sweep of the bars;

We seek then the parlor — rag-carpet on floor,
A wild staring sampler framed over the door,
Chairs yellow and bright, wooden clock ticking loud,
A mirror, whose gilding baize wraps in a shroud,
Brown hangings of paper the windows that screen,
And hearth filled with plumes of asparagus green.
The girls there await us; our path we commence
Through crimson-stemmed buckwheat, o'er rough clearing fence;
The "barrens" spread round us, a shrubby pine growth
With dwarfed sneaking hemlocks thin sprinkled, as loath
To show their thin faces, and gaunt trees with locks
Of gray brittle moss, and earth scattered with rocks.
Yet paths branch all over the cattle have trod,
The ground-pine o'ertwining its thick fringing sod,
The low whortleberries! what thousands we view,
In large tempting clusters of light misty blue!
As round them we gather and cull with delight
A sound stops the mirth, pales the cheek with affright,
A quick whizzing sound, like the wings of a bee
Shrill singing in efforts from toils to be free;
The rattlesnake! back, back — the rattlesnake! look
At his coil of fierce wrath in yon bough-shadowed nook!
His eyes flash in sparkles — his tongue quivers red,
The brown turns to bronze as he arches his head;
Back — back, still his warning the dread reptile gives,
The post he has taken he holds while he lives;
High shakes he his rattles with venomous strength,
Keep back, and no danger — he darts but his length!
A stone whizzes at him — he writhes at the blow,

More fierce is his rattle, more vivid his glow,
His eyes flash more luridly — swifter his tongue —
See, see, from his coil the fierce demon has sprung!
But another jagged missile is hurled on his head,
Down crushing its terror — his being is sped.

We come to a hill, once with trees plumaged o'er,
But a whirlwind has struck it — its pride is no more.
Strewed round, like the straw that the reaper disdains,
In a wild tangled mass lie the forest remains;
Forked roots with the soil their tough fibres had grasped,
Boughs twisted in boughs they in falling had clasped,
Trunks lying on trunks in strange mazes, but through
The path turns and winds like a labyrinth-clew,
Till we reach a great hemlock, its body stretched prone
Down the slope of the hill it once claimed for its throne;
Along its rough surface we tread as a bridge,
And leave the drear wind-fall, with joy, on its ridge.

The forest spreads over its ceiling of green,
We thread its dim aisles, its high columns between;
The wintergreens show, lying low at our tracks,
Their balls, as though moulded of pure snowy wax;
The mallows, in clumps spotted over the grass,
Their cheeses encased in their drawn sacks, we pass;
Its scarf of rich pink the wild rose-bush displays,
A canopy fit for the dance of the fays;
On its slim pillared stem hangs the sunflower's crown,
Points of delicate gold round a bosom of brown;

We strip the red beads from the sorrel, and shake
The down from the rich tawny plumes of the brake;
We part with soft click the smooth joints of the rush,
To scent their strong fragrance the mint-leaves we crush,
While the blackberry's beehive-shaped fruitage of jet
Juts cluster'd in brambles twined round like a net.
But on! for a low steady murmur is heard,
Like the pine when its plumes by soft breathings are stirred;
Then deeper and sterner, as onward we wend,
Like the pine when the breeze makes its pyramid bend,
Then swelled to an air-shaking, nerve-thrilling roar,
Like a forest of pines when the blast tramples o'er.
We haste down the steep in the serpent-like path,
Still louder the torrent's stern, breath-taking wrath,
Till we pause at the brink of a pool dark as night,
And scattered with slow circling spangles of white.
A deep gorge winds upward, and forth with a bound
The cataract's pitch shakes its thunder around;
It comes from its shadowed and prison-like glen
With a leap and a roar, like a lion from den;
Wild fir-trees, contorted as fixed in some spasm,
And tall bristling pines adding gloom to the chasm,
One grim mass of gloom, webbed below with a screen,
The cataract casting white flashes between,
As though a mad monster in torments beneath
Were now and then grasping the boughs with his teeth.

Around the black pool spread the thickets, and push
Their skirts in the water, of sapling and bush.
In June, the dense laurels that shadow the brink
Are covered with beautiful clusters of pink;
But now, in the sun their long leaves to the sight
Glint from their green polish swift glances of light.
Our party has spread into groups scattered round,
Some listening intent to the cataract's sound;
Some swinging on grape-vines slung loose between trees,
Their foreheads fanned cool in the play of the breeze;
Some kneeling where up peers a fountain of glass,
Like an eye of soft gray, through its lashes of grass;
While some climb the platform o'erjutting, where sweep
The torrent's white plunges, bold leap upon leap,
First winding, then bounding, once more and once more,
Till each voice is blent in one agony-roar.

We all are now seated on grass green and cool,
In a thicket whence glimpses are caught of the pool;
At the height of our gladness, one points at the screen,
Where a space of the foam-jewelled basin is seen;
With still, cautious hand we our net-work divide;
Leaves shake on the basin's fringed opposite side;
Two antlers are thrust forth — out stretches a head —
A deer steals to view with slow hesitant tread;
Each side he inclines a neck graceful and slim,

Then stoops his proud forehead, advances a limb;
Draws in the clear water, moves on as he drinks,
Now the flood laves his sides; ha! he flounders, he sinks!
He rises, and, snorting, strikes out with his feet,
And, bubbles round boiling, plies swift through the sheet,
With antlers on shoulder, and nose in the air,
He comes, the bright creature! in line with our lair;
He touches the bank, it is scaled with a bound,
A shake flings the glancing drops showering around,
Then catching quick sight of an ill-shrouded face,
A brown shooting streak for an instant we trace;
The next, the close forest conceals him, and deep
Each breathes a long sigh, as just wakened from sleep.

Now some all the arts of the angler employ,
The keen-sighted, quick-hearing trout to decoy:
A bright mimic fly skims the surface, but no!
Naught rises; we have but our pains for the throw;
A worm up and down next moves gently, alas!
Not a jerk to the rod, not a break on the glass,
Yet air-bells burst round us, and leapings are heard,
Except where our lines are, the whole pool is stirred;
But here comes a butterfly! follow his skim,
We 'll warrant a trout makes a dash now at him;
Confound our ill-luck! Yes, a loud-ringing splash;
A splendid two-pounder is up like a flash,
His spots fairly gleamed in his leap to the air;
Enough! and our rods are thrown by in despair.

Meanwhile a rude platform our comrades have made,
Of logs wedged together, boards over them laid;
It floats by the pool-side; hurrah, boys, a raft!
We 'll enjoy a short trip on our light buoyant craft.
The girls shrink, but yield; we all crowd on its floor;
Still it swims to our weight — we then push from the
shore;
We pole through the water, and drive as we go,
From his sun-bask, the sheathed snapping-turtle below.
Our goal is the cataract's foot; and our ear
Is filled with the roaring, more loud as more near.
A glance of the sun the white torrent has kissed,
And see! a rich rainbow is spanned o'er the mist;
The flood seems as fierce springing at us, then lost
In a high foaming hillock convulsively tossed.
Approaching too close, the raft dips in the mound,
Like a fear-maddened steed the frail thing gives a
bound,
But the impetus sends us from danger away
Unharmed, save a quick, drenching bath of the spray;
And back safe we glide, though in loudest complaint
The girls all declare they are ready to faint.
We touch the green marge; hark! a shriek shrill and
loud,
A bird with huge wings, like a fragment of cloud,
Shoots swift from the gorge, sweeps around, then on
high
Cleaves his way, till he seems a dim spot in the sky;
Then, stooping in circles, contracting his rings,
He swoops to a pine-top, and settles his wings;

An eagle, an eagle! how regal his form!
He seems fit to revel in sunshine and storm!
What terrible talons, what strength in that beak!
His red rolling eye-balls, the proud monarch speak;
He casts looks superb and majestical down,
His pine for a throne, and his crest for a crown;
He stirs not a feather, though whoopings arise,
But still flings below mute contempt at our cries;
A branch is hurled upward, whirls near him but vain,
He looks down his eloquent, glorious disdain,
Till he chooses to spread his broad pinions of gray,
And launch in majestic, slow motion away.

SCIENCE.

SCIENCE! Explorer, Teacher, Seer sublime!
Thy path, the Universe — thine empire, Time!
At thy grand look, the startled darkness flies,
And living splendors kindle earth and skies.

It is not thine to spread poetic wing
And o'er dull earth the tints of fancy fling.
Not thine with inward shaping fire to call
The breathing figure from its marble thrall,
Not thine to waken on the canvas, hues,
Sister to those imperial Autumn strews;
Thine not the charm, with Music's magic shell,
Around the soul to weave delicious spell.
No! it is thine the loftiest heavens to sweep,
Pierce the red terrors of the central deep,
Drag from its depths the shrinking, struggling star,
And chain it captive to thy conquering car;
Then trace, with lowliest eye and subtlest art,
Life's fairy process in the floweret's heart.

Thine, to unloose the sky's entangled maze,
And bid it range in order to thy gaze —
Where the sun mantles his majestic frame

In his terrific atmosphere of flame ;
Where loveliest Luna sheds on all below
The streaming silence of her silver snow ;
Where mourn the Pleiades their sister light
For long, long ages stricken from their sight ;
Star of the North, where thou, with faithful sway,
Leads the lone sailor on his surging way !
Where seas of nebulæ are faintly traced —
Within whose haze are Virgo's wings embraced —
And where again they stretch their surges dim
Till in the depths the glittering Fishes swim ;
Where Aldebaran flames with crimson hue,
And Lyra sparkles in her lovely blue ;
Where in the Cygnet stood the star whose ray
Flashed into scarlet — paled — then died away ;
Where sovereign Sirius shows his splendid gleam ;
Double Al Geiba's gold and emerald beam ;
Where Argo skims the ethereal ocean's brow
With Markeb's torchlight pouring from its prow ;
Where, bowing grandly to the passing hours,
The Southern Cross its gorgeous radiance showers,[1]

[1] "In the Spanish settlements of tropical America, the first settlers were accustomed, even as is now done, to use, as a celestial clock, the Southern Cross, calculating the hours from its inclined or vertical position. — *Humboldt's Cosmos.*

"It is a timepiece which advances very regularly nearly four minutes a day, and no other group of stars affords to the naked eye an observation of time so easily made. How often have we heard our guides exclaim in the savannahs of Venezuela, or in the desert extending from Lima to Truxillo, 'Midnight is past, the Cross begins to bend !' " — *Humboldt's Travels.*

Whose holy lights, in Dante's mystic line,
With Prudence, Justice, Strength, and Temperance
shine ;
With the alternate orbs — the Polar Three —
Blazing abroad Faith, Hope, and Charity —
The first loud launching its proud chant afar,
" Here we are Nymphs, but each in heaven a star ! "
Types of the seven great virtues — guides on earth —
But angels still in realms that saw their birth ;[1]

[1] Io mi volsi, a man destra e posi mente
All'altro polo, e vidi quattro stelle
Non viste mai fuor ch'alla prima gente."
Purgatorio 1, v. 22–24.

Humboldt in a note to his *Cosmos* says: "I have elsewhere attempted to dispel the doubts which several distinguished commentators of Dante have advanced in modern times respecting the 'quattro stelle.' To take his problem in all its completeness we must compare the passage, 'Io mi volsi,' &c., with the other passages: Purg. 1., v. 37; viii. v. 85–93; xxix. v. 121; xxx. v. 97; xxxi. v. 106, and Inf., xxvi. v. 117 and 127. The Milanese astronomer, De Cesaris, considers the three '*facelle*' ('Di che ill polo di quà tutto quanto arde,' and which set when the four stars of the Cross rise) to be Canopus, Achernar, and Fomalhaut. I have endeavored to solve these difficulties by the following considerations. The philosophical and religious mysticism which penetrates and vivifies the grand composition of Dante, assigns to all objects, besides their real or material existence an ideal one. It seems almost as if we beheld two worlds reflected in one another. The four stars represent in their moral order the *cardinal virtues*, prudence, justice, strength, and temperance; and they therefore merit the name of the holy lights, '*luci sante.*' The three stars which light the pole represent the *theological virtues*, faith, hope, and charity. The first of these beings themselves reveals their double nature, chanting, 'Here we are nymphs, in heaven we are stars;' *noi sem qui ninfe, e nel cielo semo stelle.* In the land of truth, in the terrestrial paradise, there are seven nymphs. *In cerchio faceran di se claustro le sette ninfe.* This is the union of all the cardinal and theological virtues. Under these mystic

Where the vast serpent's convolutions roll;
Where the black stars crawl, weird-like, round the pole;[1]
Where, through the orbless deserts there outspread,[2]
Sufi's White Ox and lowlier brother tread;[3]
Where, smoothed by distance to one boundless ray
Of shining sun-dust, rolls the Milky Way;—
The whole vast Universe, in sovereign thrall,
Marching around one central World of all![4]

Oh Tropic heavens, last born and issuing forth
In golden mail for conquest of the North!
The first time dawning on the Brahmin's eye
In thy strange splendors, from his colder sky![5]

forms we can scarcely recognize the real objects of the firmament separated from each other, according to the eternal laws of the *celestial mechanism*. The ideal world is a free creation of the soul, the product of poetic inspiration." — *Examen Crit.*, t. iv., pp. 324–332.

1 "The Black Specks which attracted the attention of Portuguese and Spanish pilots as early as the close of the fifteenth and the beginning of the sixteenth centuries, circle round the southern pole opposite to the Magellanic Light-clouds, although at a greater distance from it." — *Cosmos.*

2 "The larger of the two Magellanic clouds which circle round the starless, desert pole of the south." &c., &c. — *Cosmos.*

3 The larger Magellanic cloud was noticed first under the name of the White Ox by Abderrahman Sufi, an Arabian astronomer, who wrote in the middle of the tenth century.

4 Supposed to be in or near Alcyone in the centre of the Pleiades. It is also supposed that the light from Alcyone takes 500 years in passing to the earth.

5 "In a fine episode to the *Ramayana*, the oldest heroic poem of Indian antiquity, the stars in the vicinity of the south pole are declared,

Oh Tropic heavens ! what pomp superb is thine !
Man, peal thy loftiest hymn at God's sublimest shrine!
And thou whole Universe, thy Balance hung
On the Equator ! can the feeble tongue
Thy glories tell ? No ! reason, fancy prone,
Awed into naught we sink at His Almighty Throne !

How grand to dwell in Saturn, and behold
Those rings of glittering hues around him rolled ;
Drink, in far Uranus, with dazzled eye,
The pomp of moons that crowns his stately sky ;
Dash with the Comet darting on his flight,
Through all the beauty, majesty of light ;
Past, where winged Perseus wields aloft his brand ;
The star where points Andromeda her hand ;
Past sceptred Cepheus, o'er the Cygnet's wings ;
Where shows the Harp its many colored strings ;
Whirl by Bootes hounding on the Bear ;
Round the grim Lions, round the Hydra's lair ;
O'er Argo's deck — thence, mark, across the field,

for a singular reason, to have been more recently created than the northern. When Brahminical Indians were emigrating from the northwest to the countries around the Ganges, from the 30th degree of north latitude to the lands of the tropics, where they subjected the original inhabitants to their dominion, they saw unknown stars rising above the horizon as they advanced towards Ceylon. In accordance with ancient practice, they combined these stars into new constellations. A bold fiction represented the later-seen stars as having been subsequently created by the miraculous power of Visvamitra, who threatened "the ancient gods that he would overcome the northern hemisphere, with his more richly starred southern hemisphere." — *Cosmos*, note.

The rich stars flashing in thè Centaur's shield;
Thence where the Carrier holds his spangled urn,
Where in Orion's belt the diamonds burn;
Then, the all-conquering sun approaching nigh,
Feel his keen fire upon the withering eye;
Then, shooting madly from that scorching blaze,
Behold him shrink at last, a point upon the gaze.

Next to plunge downward from some shuddering height,
Down through the worlds in fierce and breathless flight,
Down, down, through dizzy depths, to other realms,
Whose very thought the reason overwhelms —
Then up the same stupendous height to scale
Where Fancy's lightning wings in staggering terrors fail.

Thou claim'st the soft Zodiacal,[1] whose gold
Owns the free Ring in neighboring ether rolled;
The wondrous region of the meteor-spray,
And where the rich Auroral splendors play;
The slumbering clouds that silver summer's air,
Or, with dread threatening, grimly blacken there;
The dry Harmattan, in its misty flight,

[1] "We may with no inconsiderable degree of probability, include within the domain of our sun, in the immediate sphere of its central force, a rotating ring of vaporous matter, lying probably between the orbits of Venus and Mars, but certainly beyond that of the Earth, which appears to us in a pyramidal form, and is known as the Zodiacal Light." — *Cosmos.*

Blinding the sun and changing all to white ;
The Stream that, rolling from its mystic source,
Breathes its own climate in its wandering course ;
The strange Magnetic currents of the globe ;
Its life-sustaining atmospheric robe ;
The drear Eclipse — the boiling Thermal flood ;
Java's death-valley ; Morat's lake of blood ;
The Caspian's burning shore ; the ceaseless fire
The Parsee worshipped on his mountain pyre ;
The moon's gray earth-light ; Twilight's lingering gleam ;
The weed-twined fields that o'er the ocean stream ;
The feathery flake ; the rainbow's lovely hues ;
The gloomy frost-smoke ; the condensing dews ;
The deadly Earthquake writhing on its path ;
The fierce Volcano bursting in its wrath ;
The welcome west-wind's sweet, caressing breath ;
The mad Tornado whirling forth in death ;
The Maelstrom lurking with its grasping grave ;
The trampling Spout — that link of cloud and wave ;
The Ocean's western march — its ebb and flow ;
The Earth's mysterious self-existent glow ;
The Phantom Vessel glimmering in the sky ;
The Brocken's Spectre, darkly reared on high ;
The crimson snow that fringes Arctic ice ;
The weird Parhelion's beautiful device ;
The wizard ball that dances on the mast ;
The fiery surges by the prow upcast ;
Locked icebergs splintering through the awful night ;
And quenchless midnight suns with their wild scarlet light.

Summits whose flint frowns back the smiling Spring,
Where dies the moss, and cowers the Condor's wing;
Slopes, where the avalanche its ambush takes,
Bursts at a breath, and down in thunder breaks;
Gulfs, where from year to year the glacier creeps;
Cloud-piercing crags the chamois only leaps;
Mountains whose thawless snows sublimely rise
In peaks, like Titans, challenging the skies,
Where the blood pauses in the blasting air,
Dauntless treads Science, searching, conquering there.
In grassy hollows where the leafy play
Weaves light and shadow from the golden day,
Where birds sing sweetly, and the diamond dew
Is sipped by winds from blooms of every hue,
There Science lingers through the hastening hours,
Delving the soils and bending o'er the flowers.

By streams that bicker in their meteor pass,
Where scaly glitterings streak the silvery glass,
There Science ponders; and where ledges rise
In varying strata, decked in differing dies,
There the light tapping of her hammer calls
The tiptoe echoes from the loosening walls;—
She parts the seam — she chains her thoughtful sight
On marks that show Time's unrecorded flight.
Where the grand billow, crumbling from its comb,
With low, rich rumble, swings away in foam,
There Science strays through weed and shell that fringe
The gleaming strand in many a rainbow tinge;

Sweeps o'er the ocean in the tempest's face,
The surge to measure, and the currents trace;
Notes where the Trades soft winnow o'er the tide,
Bearing the bark in undulating glide,
And where the black Typhoon bursts red with wrath,
Tearing the wreck it tramples in its path;
Fathoms, where countless periods have spread o'er
With dead, the deep sea's ever-growing floor;
Shows how the insect, by instinctive call,
Branches and dies — himself his flinty wall; —
Lifting the continents — the dotting isles
That dimple ocean with a thousand smiles.
Where, up from rocky, sunless depths, are cast
God's written histories of the ages past, —
Prints, that proclaim where once the monster strode,
Or swept on wings that darkened where they rode;
Signs, that display when slow progressive earth
Called the broad bannery coal-fern into birth,
Whelmed it in gloom, whence, true to Nature's plan,
Wakening in stone, it gave itself to man —
There Science pierces — there her ken perceives
The world's true records graved on deathless leaves;
Builds from a scale — a foot — complete the frame,
And even the era shows to which its life holds claim.

Glance o'er the earth — its human movements scan,
And thou, O Science! still art guide to man!
Thine is the finger, faithful through the dark,
O'er trackless wastes, to point the trusting bark;
Thine is the beacon blazing o'er the spray

To warn the wanderer of the storm away;
Thine is the tube that, like the prophet's eye,
Pierces to scenes no other can descry;
Thine is the Engine's calculating brain,
That o'er the Numeral Kingdom wields domain;
Thine the witch glass that shows how wondrous rife
The tiniest globule teems with darting life;
Thine, the light globe that navigates the air,
With flight earth-dwindling — o'er the thunder's lair;
Thine, the slight rod whose points the lightnings greet,
And draw their terrors harmless at the feet;
Thine, the grand pile that shoots the electric stream;
Thine, that illumes vast cities with its gleam;
Thine, the untiring, space-devouring car;
Thine, the strange spark that flashes thought afar;
Thine, the sun's pencil on the crystal pressed;
And thine the wafting breath o'er ocean's conquered breast.

Thine the great oak that sees slow ages pass;
The little violet dying with the grass;
The myriad tribes of air and earth and sea,
Roamers at will, yet subject all to thee!
The lofty eagle revelling in his might,
Seeking the sun in proud, unfaltering flight:
The lowly humming-bird — the feathery gem —
Flecking with opals every fragrant stem;
The fire-eyed lion filling with his fear
The sands, as if the fierce Simoom were near;
The velvet tiger of soft Ceylon's isle;

The slippery snake where Plata's blossoms smile;
The mighty whale whose ponderous gambol shocks
The deep, till, like a cork, the tall ship rocks;
The bubble nautilus, that spreads its sail
Of fairy purple, to the favoring gale.

Long shall full memory hold the scenes where late
The sons of Science met for high debate!
How on the mountain-tops of thought they strayed,
And trophies, torn from those dim heights, displayed![1]
Then, how, beneath the tent's o'ersweeping cloud,[2]
They showered their jewels to the raptured crowd!
And last, how thrilled the throng — one beating heart —
To the great Orator's resistless art!
Lighting the reason with his learning's ray,
Dazzling the fancy with his sunny play,
Charming — convincing — till his lofty theme
Became by day the thought — by night the dream.[3]

Reared by munificence transcending praise
Which DUDLEY'S name bears down to future days,
The gift of her who still survives to wear
That name thus honored by her tender care,
For whom green wreaths will Science ever twine,
Due to her offering at a blended shrine,

1 The Scientific Convention held at Albany, N. Y., in August, 1856.
2 Inauguration of the Dudley Observatory, August 28, 1860.
3 Edward Everett.

The graceful temple of the sky has birth
To scan its realms and draw them down to earth.
Proud to all future, may the structure stand —
Knowledge, in radiant streams, diffusing o'er the land![1]

[1] Dudley Observatory, Albany, N. Y.

END OF VOL. I.

www.ingramcontent.com/pod-product-compliance
Lightning Source LLC
LaVergne TN
LVHW020240110826
845151LV00003B/989

* 9 7 8 1 4 2 5 5 3 0 6 6 2 *